Praise for *The Shambhala Principle*

"In this rich and touching book, Sakyong Mipham recounts his relationship with his father, Chögyam Trungpa, to illustrate his personal journey of discovering the Shambhala principle of basic goodness and enlightened society. His contemplation of humanity's true nature invites us all to do the same: dig deep into our hearts and bring forth the jewel that will illuminate our own inherent worthiness and that of society—as well as the worthiness of the beautiful earth we inhabit. This is the love that connects us all. I hope everyone will join Sakyong Mipham in this global conversation. This is a pivotal book for our time."

—**Pema Chödrön, author of *When Things Fall Apart***

"At a time when we can either destroy the world or create a good future, Sakyong Mipham proposes to use the power of goodness to solve our problems. In this surprising and inspiring book the author develops the view that humanity at the core is basically complete, good, and worthy. If you feel sometimes overwhelmed by the daily crimes and disasters, this is a healing book and a basis for hope, one that shows how basic goodness can begin to affect our homes, workplaces, hospitals, and schools, extending all the way to our economic and political systems."   —**Lothar Schäfer, author of *Infinite Potential: What Quantum Physics Reveals About How We Should Live***

"In *The Shambhala Principle*, Sakyong Mipham offers an inspiring vision of the fundamental wisdom, grace, and courage that resides in the heart of every human being. Rich in insight and practical detail, *The Shambhala Principle* is an indispensable guide to personal and societal transformation. It is at once a moving and deeply personal tribute to his father, Chögyam Trungpa Rinpoche, and a transmission of timeless principles presented in a manner uniquely suited to the challenges of the twenty-first century."   —**Eric Swanson, coauthor of *The Joy of Living* and *Open Heart, Open Mind***

THE
SHAMBHALA
PRINCIPLE

DISCOVERING HUMANITY'S
HIDDEN TREASURE

Sakyong Mipham

HARMONY
BOOKS · NEW YORK

Copyright © 2013 by Mipham J. Mukpo

All rights reserved.
Published in the United States by Harmony Books, an imprint of the
Crown Publishing Group, a division of Random House LLC,
a Penguin Random House Company, New York.

www.crownpublishing.com

HARMONY BOOKS is a registered trademark, and the Circle colophon
is a trademark of Random House LLC.

Originally published in hardcover in the United States by
Harmony Books, an imprint of the Crown Publishing Group, a division
of Random House LLC, New York, in 2013.

Library of Congress Cataloging-in-Publication Data
is available upon request.

ISBN 978-0-7704-3745-9
eBook ISBN 978-0-7704-3744-2

PRINTED IN THE UNITED STATES OF AMERICA

Cover design by Laura Duffy

10 9 8 7 6 5 4 3 2 1

First Paperback Edition

To Humanity

contents

prologue

We humans have come to a crossroads in our history: We can either destroy the world or create a good future. Even climatically, the balance is shifting to dramatically change the face of the earth. Our ecosystem is in a precarious and fragile state, and our future depends on our actions as a species. At this time, many of us feel overwhelmed by the day-to-day. We don't have the time or energy to contemplate personal or social principles, and we may feel helpless in terms of shifting the future. How we move forward cannot depend on one spiritual tradition, economy, or political system, but rather should depend on who we feel we are, both personally and socially. What is the nature of humans and our society? In this light, human nature is the most important global issue.

The Shambhala Principle centers around a profound

transmission, a nonverbal transference of wisdom: Humanity and society are basically good. I received this wisdom from my father, Chögyam Trungpa Rinpoche, who brought the Shambhala principle to our modern world. The principle of basic goodness is not particularly religious or secular. It is about how humanity at the core is complete, good, and worthy. If we can feel confident in our goodness, it will illuminate our life and society.

This simple principle touches the inseparability of personal and social transformation: While it is true that our minds collectively shape our society, it is also true that our society shapes our minds. As our daily activities further express confidence, basic goodness can begin to affect our homes, workplaces, hospitals, and schools, extending all the way to our economic and political systems.

In this book I recollect my own experience—spiritual and hereditary—in presenting themes that might help shift our species to a bright and successful future. I feel we must awaken and have confidence in our own worthiness to be here and enrich this earth with our treasure. Yet it is challenging. Can experiencing and trusting our goodness—and that of society—alter the nature of our reality? If we all tried it, what kind of revolution would we see?

The Shambhala Principle is a reflection on my own journey, and particularly on my relationship with my father. It is based on a series of very simple dialogues during our time together in this life, regarding themes that surround humanity and society. These exchanges began to shape my understanding of profound, meaningful questions and answers about basic goodness, bravery, and creating enlightened society. Most of these dialogues did not happen in a formal setting—we would be having dinner, driving in a car, or simply sitting together for many hours in silence, punctuated only by a few words of exchange. Since the relationship with my father had many facets—father and son, teacher and student, friend and ally—these bits of wisdom did not always seem particularly serious or dramatic. At times, his comments would be accompanied by a joke or a smile.

Dialogue has long existed in ancient Greece and Asia as a way to transfer wisdom and culture. It is one of the most potent ways in which we humans learn. Using a simple exchange, a culture is being transmitted. In the case of my father, he was constantly transmitting the culture of basic goodness and good human society. Building *The Shambhala Principle* around our dialogues was a way for me to share my journey, an experience of coming to understand these themes. It is my hope that it will inspire others to contemplate them. Since we are living in a time when we are continuously inundated with different views, it is hard to know what is real and important. It is a time when we have to self-reflect in order to see what is meaningful.

The Shambhala Principle invites the reader to join me in this contemplation. Underneath the day-to-day stress, how does it feel to be human? Is there natural goodness, kindness, and strength? At this crossroads, how humanity views itself at some deep level is going to make or break the situation. Can we make the time for such a contemplation, individually and collectively? The simple act of self-reflection has the power to bring us into a more spacious environment. Out of that space, care arises naturally. As more of us feel our goodness, the future of humanity and our planet will shift.

Basic goodness can be expressed in all aspects of life. In this light, I reflect on how realizing basic goodness might affect the economy, health, and education. I do this in order to initiate a dialogue about how basic goodness can be applied to society as a whole. In this way, dialogue becomes the method of creating society through exchange, opening new pathways for exploration and development. I hope these pathways lead experts in various fields to advance this discussion.

Never before has there been a time when reflection on human nature is so important, particularly because of the power of technology. Misused, technology can isolate us, numbing our social and human tendencies while keeping us continuously occupied. Used affirmatively, it can be a powerful vehicle for allowing each of us to participate in the global community of people who wish to shift the destiny of our planet.

I am delighted to offer this guidance for the future. It

is contained in a question, a search, a discovery, and a statement about life, all reflected in conversations with my father, whose memory I wish to invoke. An undaunted social visionary, he represents the spirit of the Shambhala principle: manifesting bravery from the ground of our own goodness. This book is not intended to be a detailed exposition on the teachings of Shambhala or the Buddhist philosophy, or a presentation of Western thought or history. Rather, *The Shambhala Principle* is an attempt to contextualize and bring to light penetrating insights that my father expressed. Because his life spanned both ancient and modern, East and West, I try to reference his comments not only using traditional sources within my own culture, but correlating it with Western history and thought. Even though there are differences and discrepancies between the many philosophical systems, the majority of them surround the basic themes of human nature and the nature of society.

I have organized the book along the lines of *feeling, being,* and *touching.* We can hear logics and theories, but ultimately change and growth occur when we are touched at a human level—when we personally feel and experience something. The societal level is no different. We can be well aware of climate change and overpopulation, but what moves us is direct experience. This is why feeling our own nature, in a direct way, is so potent.

As a spiritual leader with the traditional responsibilities

of a Tibetan lama, as well as the responsibilities of leadership to a diverse modern community, I began to realize that many issues that arise in our personal lives—whether they concern spirituality, livelihood, or family—are influenced by society. Ultimately, none of us can escape the influence of our society at large. We may seek to change our lifestyle, but whether we are in the East and go West, or we are in the West and go East, as humans, we are always confronted by the basic issue of how we feel about ourselves, human nature, and society. This is precisely what my father experienced in his life and travels. Even though he came from a rich Buddhist tradition, he spent the latter part of his life emphasizing the need for humanity to feel worthy, and the truth that a good human society can be created.

The Shambhala Principle is essentially a dialogue with my father regarding these themes that were so dear to him. However, this is not an autobiography or a memoir. Rather, this book arose as I myself became a parent and began to ponder the world my child is entering. It is a message for difficult times, for the Shambhala principle challenges us to join meditative insight with social vision in order to create enlightened society. Even when society seems unenlightened, it provides an opportunity for us to recognize the potential to enlighten it. This is the social vision that my father was trying to impart. May its wisdom uplift all beings.

PART I

CREATING
ENLIGHTENED SOCIETY

BEGINNINGS

EARLY ONE MORNING, when I was about twelve years old, my father called me into his room. I knew that he had something important on his mind. As I walked in, I saw him sitting up in bed. The sun streamed gently through the window. He'd just arisen. I took a few steps toward him and bowed. He beckoned me with a loving gesture, but there was an intensity to his presence. We embraced for what seemed like a very long time. Then, gazing deeply at me, he said, "You will be the next *sakyong.*"

These words touched the very fiber of who I was—and who I would become. There was also a moment of relaxation. I felt flooded with energy and, at the same time, weighed down. I looked directly into his eyes, and in our silence I could feel something powerful being communicated, a transmission with profound implications for the rest of my life.

Sakyong is a Tibetan word that literally means "earth protector," indicating the unity of temporal and spiritual authority. It represents the principle of living one's life in order to create good human society. One exhibits bravery and goodness for the benefit of the world. In the Indian system, it is similar to a *dharmaraja*, or dharma king. It is like a *sheng huang*, or sage ruler, in the Chinese system. In the West, it could be likened to Plato's idea of the philosopher king. In the Shambhala tradition, it represents the principle of the enlightened warrior, someone who guards the earth not with the weapons of aggression, but with the armaments my father embodied: compassion, courage, and wisdom.

My father, Chögyam Trungpa Rinpoche, was a renowned meditation master, poet, scholar, artist, and ruler. He was the last of a generation of great Tibetan teachers who received the full training and education in what was then one of the greatest spiritual kingdoms on earth. His two principal teachers, Shechen Kongtrül and Khenpo Gangshar, were brilliant luminaries. They were not only profoundly deep meditators; they were also philosophers and scholars. My father was their primary pupil, and they transmitted to him the most sacred ancient teachings of the past twenty-five hundred years.

Most important, they passed along to him the highest of Buddhist tantras—a teaching known as the Great Perfection, which teaches that at the highest level of awareness and experience, the nature of relative and absolute are the same, a place of non-locality where time and space dissolve into each other.

My father was a descendant of Gesar of Ling, a warrior king of Eastern Tibet who brought about harmony—overcoming aggression and establishing peace. The brave and heroic Gesar believed in the goodness of humanity and was able to raise the spirits and energy of his people at a time when they were experiencing confusion and chaos from internal and external aggressors. Thus, my father held the ancestral bloodline of not only warriorship, but royalty as well.

In this rich and ancient culture, a unique mixture of harsh climate and deep, meditative self-reflection, my father was brought up to trust that human nature was good, and that society can manifest this goodness. As the spiritual leader and ruler of the Surmang region in Eastern Tibet, he was well versed in spiritual and temporal matters, in constant contact with the follies and virtues of human behavior. However, he always remained strong in his principle of relying on basic goodness in conducting his affairs.

Given the speed and aggression of our world and the tenuous state of our ecosystem, it appears that humanity has forgotten its innate goodness. Yet despite degradation, cruelty, and a life constantly inundated with anger and jealousy, human goodness does remain intact, hidden within. It was my father's wish to remind humanity that it is good.

As a young man, my father was an extraordinarily gifted individual. Not only was he able to assimilate the vast and complex knowledge that existed in Tibet at that time, but he also became renowned for having prophetic visions and insight about future occurrences. He even predicted the fall of Tibet, which later helped direct his escape, in which he led hundreds of others over the Himalayas into India.

Because of his stature, keen intelligence, and deep visions, my father was constantly asked to give advice to high lamas and kings, as well as to the lay community. With his perpetual blend of deep spiritual insight and daily worldly affairs, what began to arise was a vision of an enlightened human society that had at its core the acknowledgment and recognition of humanity's goodness. These visions arose, inspired by the legendary kingdom of Shambhala, the land of peace, happiness, and prosperity. As my father contemplated the nature of humanity and society, he began to compose texts that filled many volumes. These later became known as the "treasure teachings" of Shambhala.

Then, during the invasion of Tibet, my father witnessed

firsthand the cruel and savage behavior of a people who had become consumed with aggression, having lost touch with their basic goodness. Towns, villages, and monasteries were destroyed. Monks, nuns, and friends were tortured and killed. In 1959, the violence rose to such intensity that he finally fled his homeland. Having been a ruler—a symbol of temporal and spiritual authority—he became a refugee, a man without home or country.

Being forced to leave his home and venture into a great, unknown world, my father began to ponder the notions of human nature and society altogether. It was during his escape, high in the Himalayas, as he gazed onto the great plains of India, that a vision to create an enlightened human society, a network of wisdom and kindness, arose. Such a society would honor and encourage innate goodness, and cultivate the wisdom in all cultures and traditions. He felt that the essential ingredient to create such a society was bravery. This bravery had the inherent quality of not giving up on humanity. At the same time, in order to do this, he realized that he had to be expansive and open-minded.

This Shambhala vision of enlightened society—as he later called it—revealed to him how a good human society could occur, and it happened at the same time that his ancient culture was being destroyed. His inspiration about enlightened society was not to re-create Tibet, for he had reflected intimately on the shortcomings of his own culture. Rather, he was harnessing the deep wish for a good society that has existed throughout the evolution of humanity. The deep, strong, and palpable desire that humanity exist on earth in a good and dignified manner became the focus of his life. He engaged his intelligence, heart, and exertion in order to bring about this profound inspiration.

My father's vision of enlightened society was not a utopian fantasy, nor was his wish for humanity to live in harmony born from a naïve understanding of worldly affairs. It came out of witnessing the horrors of human savagery. Because he had witnessed human degradation at such an intimate level, his desire to create a good society is a testament to his character and a reflection of his ability to forgive, comprehend, and assess. Thus, the source of this social vision was the durable quality of the human heart.

My father's visions inspired him to pursue a Western education with the express purpose of trying to create enlightened society. He learned English in India, and in 1963 he traveled to England to study at Oxford University, where he delved into the rich tradition of Western philosophy and comparative religion. He studied theology and took great interest in the Japanese arts, including flower arranging and calligraphy. His homelessness and exile had become a journey of discovery and assimilation.

This is not to say that it was easy losing his friends, his home, and his country. There were moments of great uncertainty and times when he was actively questioning his own identity. When he arrived at Oxford, my father was still wearing traditional Tibetan robes. Ironically, the tradition he represented, which was full of authenticity dating back thousands of years, was now considered off-beat. Purely due to the reality of a new environment, this venerated figure of spiritual authority became a marginalized and suspicious individual, typecast and misunderstood. He told me that people would not ask "Who are you?" but "What are you?" He would reply, "I am a human being."

With his complete reversal of fortune, having experienced both the cruelty and the cynicism of humanity, my father might well have begun to doubt the Shambhala principle of basic goodness. This would have been understandable and even appropriate. It would have been his right to conclude that human life is solitary, poor, nasty, brutish, and short, as Hobbes and other philosophers have done. Yet even through dark times, my father maintained his conviction in basic goodness. Indeed, his transcultural journey made him even more determined to proclaim that message for this particular age of doubt and cynicism.

For the rest of his life, my father worked to awaken others to basic goodness. He was a major force in introducing Tibetan Buddhist teachings to the modern world, but he was not content simply being classified as a spiritual teacher. Rather, he felt that his calling was to be a sakyong, "earth protector," and to help humanity as a whole. Thus, he introduced the teachings on Shambhala warriorship, which emphasize connecting to our humanity, recognizing our inherent goodness, and communicating through kindness and bravery as a means to establish a good, enlightened human society.

As my father gazed deeply at me on that morning, I realized in that pivotal moment that he was asking me to take responsibility for this profound vision that was so dear to his heart—the core of his being. The vision that had sustained him throughout his dramatic and tumultuous life—this most innate desire to live in a good human society—he was now asking me to hold as an earth protector.

Since that pivotal interaction with my father, I, too, have traveled a challenging and at times difficult path to understand and come to terms with human nature. Not dissimilar to my father's, in my journey the principle of basic goodness has been tested as I have experienced the suffering and aggression of the world that we live in. In realizing my duty as an earth protector—to protect the character of humanity against doubt and losing heart—I have drawn the conclusion that to protect this earth is to protect the very spirit of life.

Within humanity is goodness that is alive and fully intact but, in these times, it is surrounded by the darkness of uncertainty and fear. If, by taking a moment to self-reflect, we realize the preciousness of our life and our connection with others, we can begin to feel the goodness that has sustained us throughout all time. In this seemingly insignificant moment when we feel our own goodness, a seismic shift occurs. Liberated of doubt regarding our nature, we see a vast, new horizon of human possibility.

During the fifth century B.C.E., the Buddha and Socrates roamed the earth and came to their own conclusions regarding the innate goodness of humanity. For some reason, humanity does not draw this conclusion very often. Because humanity is now at a critical juncture—a crossroads at which we are deeply contemplating the nature of our planet and of our species—we must draw our conclusion carefully. Our economic volatility and the many natural disasters we are experiencing are wake-up calls.

Even spiritually we are at a crossroads. Because of the perpetual play of interdependence and impermanence, it is very unlikely that a world as big and unruly as ours will ever be dominated or united by one spiritual tradition. We must support the unique qualities of various traditions, for that is the fabric of humanity. Its diversity and intricacy keep us strong, like nature itself. At the same time, if we are bound by a unifying principle, humanity will feel like one family. The Shambhala principle of basic goodness has that power.

2

THE SHAMBHALA PRINCIPLE

Although deep inside I had known from a very early age that to be the sakyong was my role in life, once my father made it formal, I realized that I wasn't really certain what it meant to be a sakyong. When I asked my father what the sakyong did, he replied, "The sakyong wakes people up to their own basic goodness."

That's it? I thought. Being a sakyong couldn't possibly be that simple, could it? What did he mean that people are basically good? And if that were true, why was there so much suffering? This was a koan, a contemplation of sorts. Little did I know at the time that I would spend the next thirty-five years of my life searching to understand—and experience—the simplicity and complexity of what my father taught me.

My father wanted my studies to mirror his own education later in his life, to reflect a balance of East and West. I received the spiritual inheritance of my own tradition, with its deep esoteric wisdom, studying Buddhist philosophy and teachings of tantra. Over the years, I was also introduced to Western thought, philosophy, politics, and economics, as well as poetry and literature. Physically I trained in archery, horsemanship, and martial arts. Thus my education was both classical and modern. In addition, I practiced meditation and contemplation in both Asia and the West. My training and practice taught me that studying itself does not lead to wisdom. Rather, by self-reflecting, I needed to internalize what I had learned, try it out in my daily life, and then reflect on the outcome. That is the process that leads to wisdom.

I was vaulted into an even deeper internal process by the passing of my father in 1987. I was twenty-four at the time, and losing him was a time of great pain and confusion, not only for me but also for the Shambhala community and the world. As his spiritual heir, it was my job to succeed him. Yet I felt neither ready nor capable of following in his footsteps. I was still young, and I needed to forge my own spiritual path. The way ahead of me seemed unknown and foreboding. Still, from a sense of duty—and a deep love for my father—I continued studying, practicing Buddhism, and attempting to walk the Shambhala path of warriorship.

At times, this period was difficult and challenging. Not only was I deepening my spiritual understanding; I was being asked to lead a large and diverse community, both in the East and West. Simultaneously, I was dealing with people's loss, insecurities, anger, and confusion. In addition to all this, I felt the huge responsibility of holding a lineage that dated back thousands of years; it was now up to me to determine how it should move forward. I had to not only understand the essence of my own tradition, but also determine how to continue it within the context of the modern culture. I was constantly being tested, within both my own community and the world in general. At times, people encouraged me not to be concerned with the general plight of the world, but to focus on my own tradition. However, as I continued in my leadership role, I began to realize that in both spiritual and secular endeavors, the notion of human nature kept arising, and I was challenged daily to contemplate basic goodness.

During this period I often pondered my father's desire to go beyond the confines of his own spiritual borders and enter the world of global economic, political, and environmental concerns. Simply presenting himself as a Tibetan Buddhist lama and teacher would have been safer and less complicated. However, that is not who my father was. Most important, that is not who he felt he was. His teachers had told him that the world they knew and loved was coming to an end, and that it was up to him to transmit the essence of Tibet's wisdom—that people and society are good—beyond the parameters of Buddhism, or any religion. He saw that the best way to do this was to assume his role as an earth protector, protecting the goodness by awakening others to it.

I asked myself, Why would such a brilliant individual highlight as simple a message as basic goodness?

My father was a great believer in humanity. In both the East and the West, he was always synthesizing the knowledge that he had gained, seeking to understand and compare not only what the Buddha had taught, but also the teachings of Plato, Aristotle, Jesus, and those of Judaism and Islam, as well as the great minds of China—Lao Tzu and Confucius. He particularly respected India's great ruler King Ashoka, as well as Dogen of the Zen tradition and Shotoku Taishi of Japan. As diverse as these traditions are, each of them could be reduced in size but concentrated in intensity, to encapsulate two simple ideas: Humanity is good, and good is the nature of society.

It was through study and reflection that I began to sense an inner shift in my understanding that the Shambhala principle is an underlying universal theme that exists throughout obvious and not-so-obvious threads of human thought. This universality is not a watering down of any tradition; it is the nucleus at the heart of all tra-

THE SHAMBHALA PRINCIPLE } 17

dition. It is not something we create. It is something we discover.

The word *Shambhala* means "source of happiness," and as I mentioned earlier, it is the name of a central Asian kingdom—also known as "Shangri-La"—said to have existed in the fifth century B.C.E. In the ancient Buddhist texts, it is often referred to as "Shambhala of the North." For my father, Shambhala was synonymous with the principles of courage and goodness.

The lore of Shambhala says that it was a physical country on earth, and that its citizens reached such a profound understanding of basic goodness that they attained enlightenment together. Legend has it that at that moment the entire kingdom transcended the physical bonds of the material world. Some say that Shambhala still exists, manifesting in a realm slightly beyond the grasp of our conceptual mind.

It is said that Shambhala was located at the western part of the Orient and the eastern part of the Occident—the confluence of the Asian, European, and Arabic worlds. Thus, even geographically, Shambhala was located in a position of universality. The citizens of Shambhala were said to be technologically advanced and incredibly intelligent. To create enlightened society, they roused their goodness and projected it into their daily lives, which in turn became a constant support for this enlightenment. They infused their relationships with kindness and compassion, and they also used them to develop those qualities. This all arose from a communal belief in humanity's inherent wisdom. That is why my father drew inspiration from the legend: At the confluence of these great cultures, the spirit of goodness was extolled and celebrated. It was the epitome of human realization and cultural achievement.

Shambhala is not only a place; it is a spiritual path, what is sometimes called "a worldly path" because our confidence in basic goodness allows us to relax with our world and see its sacred quality. Even in an ordinary sense, when we appreciate something, that means we have allowed ourselves to relax and take it in. When my father saw Shambhala, he was demonstrating a meditative ability. With such pure perception, he could see that individuals and society are enlightened now. Based on today's headlines, we may not be able to even imagine that, but seeing society as enlightened is a practical approach, for there is no other world, and no escape from this one.

At the same time, enlightened society is not a utopia, but a place where we are brave enough to see—and be— just who we are, surrendering our fantasies of something better. When we do that, the discovery of our own goodness on this planet becomes an exercise in appreciation and wonderment. Slowing down to self-reflect and feel our worthiness, and to feel confidence in it, creates space.

Then we have the actual intelligence to know which way to go.

Yet, lulled to sleep by surface pleasures—and horror—most of us lack confidence in basic goodness. Daily life is challenging, and there are plenty of opportunities to think human nature is bad. In the practice of self-reflection, we ask the question, How do we *feel*? When we connect with our heart, what do we find? No matter how difficult and painful life may be, basic goodness is undiluted by conditions, for it cannot change. Obstacles and challenges may arise, but they do not reduce the enlightened qualities at our disposal. If enough of us can feel our goodness, then, in a period of difficulty, society will not break down but actually become stronger.

Earlier, I mentioned the process of social illumination. That is keenly illustrated by the story of how Shambhala became an enlightened society. It is said that the first king of Shambhala, Dawa Sangpo, "Good Moon," went to the Buddha and requested wisdom so powerful that he could attain enlightenment without being forced to abandon his kingdom. Dawa Sangpo said, "With my many responsibilities, I do not have the luxury to retire to a monastery to seek personal enlightenment. Can you give me spiritual teachings I can use in daily life to bring peace and harmony to myself, my subjects, and my kingdom?"

The Buddha replied that indeed he could offer such

teachings on using society as a spiritual path, but that only a very powerful individual could accomplish them. However, the mind of Dawa Sangpo was so clear that even as the Buddha was bestowing those teachings, Dawa Sangpo understood them. Then he returned to Shambhala to teach. At that time, there were conflicting factions within the society, but after Dawa Sangpo began to teach, the entire kingdom was unified in goodness. Once people woke up to the goodness in themselves, they were able to see it in one another, and their society was naturally enlightened.

Socially and politically, the world needs the light of Shambhala right now. Imagine what could happen if we all began to feel that we are good, and that society is good—and to have confidence in ourselves that way. When I am teaching in the West, people talk about self-loathing and self-aggression. That is coming from a sense of unworthiness. There seems to be a lot of evil in the world, and many of us experience great skepticism about human nature. In addition, we may have been taught at home, school, or church that simply by having been born, we are inherently faulty or incomplete. Without a feeling of worthiness, human society and communication naturally become vehicles of manipulation and deception, and we use every activity to shore ourselves up or to outdo someone else. Through this false sense of power, life becomes a perpetual unfolding of doubt, which only confirms the inadequacies we perceive and elicits a feeling of alienation. My father called it "the setting sun." This term describes a time when humanity's sense of dignity and purpose is diminishing, like sunlight at the end of the day. What is setting is our ability to recognize our goodness.

If humanity is to survive—and not only that, to flourish—we must be brave enough to find our wisdom and let it shine. We uncover it by beginning to examine our assumptions. We may never before have considered human nature, but in order to move forward as a global community, it is vital that we do it now. Is it really our nature to be fearful and aggressive, or could it be that we are actually gentle and fearless at heart? Underneath the stress and anxiety, is it possible there is peace? If our self-reflection turns up an inkling of that, we can draw power from it, daring to shift our destiny. In this way, the Shambhala principle is a socially transformative process through which confusion about human nature becomes confidence in human worthiness.

We are living in a world where global leadership in many fields is clearly necessary. To be in the vanguard, we need to understand that the purpose of being here is to engender true peace. It is not confusion that we need, but wisdom. The wisest thing to do is to realize and cultivate our nature. Let us make that primordial stroke, mixing courage with wisdom.

I know, as did my father before me, that at this time of speed, depression, and technological absorption, it is not easy to experience such a subtle feeling, yet it is always here. Still, a question lingers: Why do we all doubt this goodness?

3

ESSENTIAL INSTRUCTIONS

ASKING MY FATHER to tell me about basic goodness often led to poetry. He would compose a poem, or ask me to. Sometimes he would snap his fingers, or smile, or touch my heart with some other gesture. Sometimes he would simply gaze at me. In the highest Buddhist teaching, these are known as essential instructions. In such transmissions, the student is introduced to profound topics, such as love, emptiness, luminosity, and compassion, which are really beyond description. Poetry, art, or gesture is used, because beyond intellectual understanding, each allows feeling to arise.

Before receiving such transmissions, at the preliminary levels of my study, I had to do the hard work of memorizing or analyzing ancient texts on emptiness, bliss, and other profound topics, so I could become familiar with how the masters had understood human nature. This course of study also involved discussion and debate. The point of the exercise was to become so familiar with the facets of human nature that I could make them my own and articulate my understanding. Aristotle and Plato also point to a need for the student to study and train in order to embody the truth. Just as in the Tibetan system, the ancient Greeks used study and dialogue to help the student make the transition from concept to experience.

At the beginning, it is challenging to experience the nature of things, because our minds are usually captivated by how things appear; we do not think about their nature, nor do we perceive it. The Shambhala tradition uses the image of a mirror to communicate the all-accommodating quality of basic goodness. The mirror is known as "cosmic" because it reflects everything. "Cosmic" surpasses conventional notions, including space and time; thus the nature of things is considered to be primordial and beyond time. The images in the mirror are inseparable from the mirror itself, like the sky melting into an early-morning lake. Thus the cosmic mirror reflects the underlying wisdom of the world, which includes everything and is perpetually arising within great openness.

My father told me that basic goodness is not simply a human phenomenon, or something that is experienced only in deep meditation. Rather, it is alive, humming through the universe as an elemental energy that is very ordinary. He would often use being outdoors as a way to introduce me to the nature of things. We would sit on the earth where we could smell the grass, feeling the wind and the warmth of the sun, and watch the clouds float by. Sometimes we worked in the garden—digging, watering, and touching the soil and plants. The garden allows us to connect with the seasons. It is a constant reminder of nowness, as the plants are always reacting to the weather and the seasonal changes.

As I grew to experience what he was teaching me, my understanding of basic goodness became less conceptual and more experiential. I began to see that while earth, air, fire, and water have different qualities, and how they manifest is always changing, their essence is the same, like sunlight sparkling on a diamond. There's a tremendous range of communicative power within these elements. Communication is a two-way street that runs on harmony. Everybody has a different face and a different shape, but somehow our hearts are all very similar. Expressing with our heart, while understanding that we all have the same heart, creates the harmony to help people realize their wisdom and compassion. The end result is freedom.

Many languages and cultures speak of this fresh feeling and the confidence that arises from our conviction in it. The great Chinese sage Mencius referred to the nature of humanity as an innate benevolence, a full human-heartedness brimming with love and altruism. In the opening lines of the *Nichomachean Ethics*, Aristotle writes, "The good has been rightfully declared to be that at which all things aim." The fourteenth-century master Longchenpa—one of Tibet's most illustrious saints—said, "Since all things are all-good, with not a single thing that is not good, all things are identical within the completely good state, in which there is neither good nor bad."

When I was first introduced to basic goodness, I had to memorize the qualities—that it was unchanging, beginningless, endless, and all-inclusive. After each definition, there would also be subcategories. Our true nature expresses itself as intelligence, clean energy, mindfulness, presence, and intuition. It also has an element of knowledge. Likewise, all external knowledge is here to wake up the basic goodness in us, for inherently we humans are knowing creatures. Unlike information, basic goodness cannot be transmitted, but only pointed out. The heart must wake up to what is already there. When we recognize and trust our primordial nature, we have confidence; we are warriors whose bravery is to hold open hearts and minds and offer these to the world. When we doubt our nature, we are cowards who hide from the world, afraid to acknowledge the openness at the root of our being. This is the choice we face.

Humanity is constantly experiencing its core open-ness through thoughts of curiosity, love, understanding—and even sadness or pain. Because we are alive, these deep-seated feelings are always bubbling up, connecting us to the world through our senses. By focusing the mind and feeling the heart, we increase our ability to connect with goodness. So we take a moment to gather our senses into our heart and feel what it means to be worthy. That ignites confidence, the spark of awakened energy. Our life is illuminated by this healthy glow.

When we touch our own energy, we become available to experience the energy of the environment. We see that the world is alive with the tangible, elemental energy of *windhorse*—the uncontrived spirit of life. Once we are aware of this steady force of wakefulness, we can always be connecting with it. Our interdependent relationship with the environment is also an expression of enlightened society. Each moment presents the opportunity to wake up to our life by tuning in with our sense perceptions: to really taste our food, for example, or to hear the sound of thunder.

When my father moved to the West, he noticed that sometimes we think that in order to be "spiritual," we need to shut down our sense perceptions. He said, "We feel we have to convert them into some sort of mythical idea of what things should be like." When we shut down our sense perceptions, we grow numb to our natural energy and disengage from our life. We tend to become heady—intellectually and emotionally isolated from the environment—and we lose the capacity to feel. Without feeling, we are no longer fully being on this planet, because we have lost the capacity to care. This is how kindness and compassion start to wane. To proceed down this road is a tragedy of astronomical proportions.

My father said, "Any perception can connect us to reality properly and fully." *Now* announces itself through our sense of touch, taste, sight, sound, and smell. What are you smelling right now? When we appreciate our senses fully, this is the moment when goodness is being expressed. Each moment feels fresh: We connect with how things are. Red is red, and a racehorse is a racehorse. We have heard about basic goodness, but after encountering it viscerally, we feel that it is true.

What is the purpose of investigating the elusive theme of human nature? My spiritual training and my reading of the works of great philosophers have shown me that we cannot underestimate the power of the mind's feeling about itself. In fact, our current modern mind is a long compilation of philosophical, economic, and spiritual views and experiences that date back centuries. Beginning in the archaic period, the ancient Greeks offered a variety of views on human nature, but there was an overall tendency to emphasize virtue. According to Aristotle, cultivating virtue was the true orientation of humanity.

There was something innate about our own movement toward goodness, even if it took hard work. The result of such virtue was good politics. The Romans also considered virtue to be the heart of a good human life. With Christianity, many questions about human nature arose. Are we innately divine—made in God's image—or are we originally sinful? To this day, various theologians continue to debate these views. During the Middle Ages, the views of ancient Greece and Rome mixed with Christian thought. Then, with the birth of modern philosophy, science, and the use of empirical investigation, which led to the Renaissance and Enlightenment, human beings gradually became the center of the universe. Yet it was unclear if this rational, modern human was basically good or basically confused.

For a while, perhaps, modern thought and technology appeared to be creating a better world, and there was a sense of celebration, evolution, and progress. Yet simultaneously, colonial power spread throughout the globe, often bringing with it violence and suffering. Was this the spread of wisdom and progress, or the spread of greed and aggression? The nature of humanity was often unclear. Great weapons of destruction were created and humanity's spirit took a tremendous blow with the occurrence of the two World Wars and the Holocaust. The sense of certainty in modernity and progress was severely challenged. During that time, various political powers arose, such as Marxism, totalitarianism, and new expressions of democracy—each trying to create what it saw as a better world. Now, in our modern era, the influence of capitalism and technology is all-pervasive.

Throughout this epic historical journey, we can trace various views regarding human nature. However, after this entire history, the view that now predominates stems from certain philosophies that assume that humanity is innately selfish. Thus, our modern minds are evolutions and compilations of all these thoughts and feelings.

It is important to acknowledge that what we consider to be human nature is the result of all the ideas and experiences of this long history. This is good news, because it gives us the opportunity to reflect together and inquire if these ideas about our nature are true to our own experience or not.

The modern identity is complex, but we all rise in the morning and wonder, Where is my place in the universe? Who and what we feel we are is an attitude that we embody from the moment we arise, throughout the entire day, and even in our sleep. Collectively, our self-identity creates our culture, and the particular social ceremonies we observe reinforce our attitude. The Shambhala principle gives us a method by which to take a fresh look, feel our own hearts, and discover for ourselves who we are.

We need to understand that no one is telling us how to feel. However, in order to come to our own conclusion about the nature of humanity, we need to let ourselves feel. When we feel goodness, a shift occurs: We get curious, which sparks care. We begin to see goodness happening in so many ways—rational and irrational, visible and invisible, and through signs, words, and examples. From that arise virtues like patience, exertion, and generosity.

Over the centuries, "virtue" has taken on a moralistic tone, and many of us are no longer drawn to the word. It may seem feeble in the wake of a collective self-identity that has bought into the belief that humanity is primordially flawed. Not only is that view demoralizing for individuals and society; it is also demoralizing for the human spirit—like telling children that they are bad from birth, and that they will never be any better. It implants a sense of futility. However, in my tradition, "virtue" doesn't have a heavily moralistic or religious overtone. It is simply what we need to create an enlightened society—a daytime star that everyone can see.

When my father had me compose poetry and walk in nature, he was teaching me that as a human being, I always have the ability to connect with goodness through my senses. He was showing me that if I practiced doing this—allowing my mind to break free from the realm of thought and logic—I would discover other modes of understanding and knowledge, such as curiosity and care. I had to move the energy from my head to my heart. Then, with confidence in my own humanity, I could relax and trust my life. As my father put it, "It unlocks something held prisoner for a very long time." That is how I discovered that life is constantly offering the transmission of basic goodness.

4

CREATION VS. DESTRUCTION

ONE MORNING AS my father and I ate breakfast, I asked him, "Do you think that the whole of society could actually become enlightened?" He looked at me and said that was not necessarily the point. There is always a natural interplay between enlightened and unenlightened, societal yang and yin. Like the knife and the sharpening stone, humanity will always be rubbing up against its unenlightened habits. "However," he said, "by creating enlightened society, we are *not* creating unenlightened society."

When my father used this word *create*, he was indicating that essentially we do not have a choice. Whether we regard society as an unfortunate burden or a valuable gift and opportunity, we are already participating in creating it. Either we are participating in a positive sense, or in a negative sense, depending on our outlook. When we are participating in a positive sense, we are fully engaged in our intention and our activity, doing good. When we are participating in a negative sense, we are not quite sure about our intention, and we are using the setting-sun edge—our doubt in basic goodness—to keep ourselves a little distant or even hostile. We go through the motions of our life, but we're just pretending. In describing this un-enlightened society, my father said, "We pretend to eat our food, wear our clothes, and put up our hair—but in whatever we do there is always the notion that everything is half-done. There is no sense of dignity at all."

Then he smiled and whispered, "Of course, we can overcome this by raising windhorse." Windhorse is the energy of the present moment, which contains this force because it is the only time we can feel basic goodness.

Once I understood how enlightened society is constantly dancing with unenlightened society like this, even in my own life, I began to see enlightened society in a different way. I realized that it is all about nurturing the human spirit—waking up to the goodness, kindness, and strength that we already have.

To put it another way, the fact that our society is experiencing a high level of fear and doubt is a signal for humanity not to give up, but rather to engage further with our enlightened tendencies. We could try patience instead of anger, goodwill instead of envy, generosity instead of grasping. If this sounds ridiculous in today's world, that's because in an unenlightened and confused society, we tend to believe in the power of negativity. But even negativity has the power to wake us up. Therefore, the more unenlightened society gets, the more powerful is the possibility of enlightening it. To experience dawn, one needs darkness. When we don't understand who we are at the core, our minds can become so dark that we become desperate to wake up. For this very reason, my father saw the power of these particular teachings for our age.

While an unenlightened society is always possible, rather than being depressed or overwhelmed by it, we can use periods of deep social degradation as reminders of our good fortune in being alive and in a situation where we can uplift ourselves and others. We can use that setting-sun edge as a constant reminder to keep our inspiration to nurture the positive. That is how humans move forward, and it is natural for us. In fact, like birds, we cannot move backward. This is not blind faith, but genuine resilience and healthiness.

When my father would use this phrase "creating enlightened society," he was often met with skepticism. I found this reaction both puzzling and understandable. He inspired a generation of people who were looking for a better future. Like them, he was a product of the modern conflicts, born just before the Second World War. There was for his generation a rising mistrust in anything organized—not only in religion but in society as a whole. The tendency of our society became not to create, but to deconstruct. We still live in a time when criticism and analysis prevail, bringing people and power structures up—and then down. We focus on people's weaknesses instead of their strengths. Any attempts at creating something—even a plan for protecting the planet—are likely to be undermined. I feel like my father used the word *create* to counter this current tendency to dismantle. It was his way of saying, "Don't give up," trying to bolster humanity's confidence in its ability to create a better world. Rather than collapsing under the seemingly overwhelming negative aspects of human behavior, this was a time to persevere. Even though he acknowledged human weaknesses, it was time for humanity to rise to the occasion.

Focusing on humanity's weaknesses is not necessarily a wise tactic for safeguarding against future tyranny or building a better world. However, the outlook of our age has been not necessarily to create a better world, but to safeguard the one we have. Our tools have been capitalism and communism, the chief powers of the last century. Capitalism generally caters to the individual and the self, while communism is rooted in a social agenda. When the Berlin Wall fell, capitalism was declared the victor. Since that time, political policies have been directed toward eradicating totalitarian threats and implementing democracies as a way to guard against tyranny. However, brutal regimes still arise, and there is great asymmetry in the relationship between wealth and poverty in the democratic societies. It has been said that the wealth in the world is now in the fewest hands than ever before, despite the attempts to implement democracy.

Along with this uncertainty about human nature, a mandate to create a better world occurred with the formation of the United Nations, as well as numerous non-governmental organizations. In the realm of economics, humanity has created corporations and businesses that dominate our society. At the same time, many wonder about the benefit of such structures. With the rising strength of corporations, governments become focused on policy-making and underwriting corporate objectives, and their power to govern is brought into question. All of this demonstrates the ongoing struggle to realize a vision for a good society.

Because the overall direction of the world is so overwhelming, many of us just participate in what we know or what is comfortable or, out of frustration, we simply try to tear everything down. But deconstructing or destroying things does not mean that something better will necessarily come about. Condemning things does not necessarily require insight or fortitude. On the other hand, the act of creation takes thoughtfulness, patience, and bravery.

Ancient Greek democracy was powered by the forward-moving energy of *arête*—"virtue and excellence"—which resulted in success and inspiration. Later, when democracy arose during the Enlightenment, seeded first by Voltaire and Rousseau, then by Franklin and Jefferson, it was not simply as the means to take down burdensome regimes in France and America. Rather, it came from the desire to create something new. These two democratic movements came into being as a result of celebrating humanity, as opposed to fearing humanity. This spirit of illumination and self-possession—seeing society's faults as well as its potential—is how any great society is born.

The principle of democracy is a call for all beings to have the freedom of equal participation in choosing their leadership and laws, but now there is a tendency to dampen that spirit. Geopolitically, we tend to use democracy just as a way to make it seem that we all have a say. But we should genuinely look to see if this is true. We do have a vote, but is that democracy's only meaning? The evolution of democracy has allowed us further participation and influence in formulating our world and society. In order for this spirit of participation to truly mold our future, we cannot simply use it as a form of protectionism. Rather, we must use it as a tool for creating a brighter future.

In recent wars and conflicts, we have seen all too well the aftermath of humanity's gruesome streak. Will attempting to protect humanity from itself allow us to move forward? If humanity is to learn from its mistakes, we need inspiration and vision about the future. With the social agenda and political process of deconstruction without creation, we lower the bar in terms of engaging human potential. Downgrading human possibility, we do not particularly eliminate evil. Rather, we give evil a weaker opponent.

If we hold the belief that humanity has already failed, and try to limit the damage with a mediocre social vision, we are surrendering to an underlying belief that humanity is bad. When we stop believing in humanity's possibilities, we stop building our future. If we have the bravery to proclaim basic goodness and move beyond our doubt about humanity, it will be harder for evil to arise.

Rousseau wrote about human goodness, kindness, and tenderness. Even though these attributes are hard to qualify, they are essential for human success and survival. Because we do not recognize and feel our own tenderness, we abuse ourselves and others, and a deep feeling of hurt begins to arise. This hardens into disappointment, discontent, discord, and, finally, anger and aggression.

Tyrants do not arise because humans are by nature evil, but because society does not acknowledge human goodness. When individuals do not know their goodness, negative tendencies begin to stir. If our whole social premise is based on paranoia about tyrants and terrorists creating havoc, we are fostering an environment of suspicion and fear in which even more individuals will become disenfranchised from good human society. Guarding the world with a safety net of deconstructionism and neutrality, we are not necessarily eliminating any human threats. Rather, our policy of disempowerment is stirring the pot of human discontent.

My father had experienced firsthand the insanity of humanity. He had felt the brunt of a violent regime. Within this context, I was struck by his careful use of *create*. He did not react with fear and hopelessness and simply say, "Never will we try again." Nor did he come to the modern world to teach us that humanity should be regarded with great cynicism, and that we should deconstruct all power bases.

Rather, he asked, What about the ability to help others? After some reflection, he concluded that humanity must raise its social consciousness, see the big picture, and strive for a good human society. He suggested that rather than participate in society by dismantling— or alternatively, by not participating at all—instead we should create something better. He felt that enlightened society depended mostly on empowering people on a human-to-human basis, independent of any particular political structure or religion: He had witnessed the pitfalls of most of them.

My father was a great advocate of some of the themes that arose from the Enlightenment—in particular, that we all have the right to freedom and justice. We should not only have freedom of speech; we should also have freedom of listening. That would mean listening with our ears, not our lips. We cannot have a more enlightened society if our habitual dynamic is a matter of one person, religion, or government trying to force itself upon another. If a more enlightened society is to come about, it must be based on a global conversation, an exchange in which we all act as spiritual and worldly conduits for the universally positive traits of humanity. This exchange must be grounded in an attitude of respect.

By saying hello, we acknowledge the existence of another. As in Africa and the world over, saying hello means, "I see you," and "You exist." This greeting is a way that humanity engenders respect. As the conceptual, material world increases its hold on us, and inanimate objects become more lifelike, we humans must become more *human*. Open hearts, kindness, and care—these are our most precious gifts. When we fail to appreciate them, enhance them, and offer them to others, we are abusing our own race. And if we do not appreciate the sensitivity and subtlety of the human heart, how can we appreciate the sensitivity and subtlety of the natural world? At this very intimate level, environmental degradation begins.

Enlightened society arises from the ground of appreciation. When humanity comes to its senses, literally, we can use them to tune into ourselves, other people, and the environment. This is what my father meant by "enlightenment." If we value a particular political or economic system above embodying our own nature, we will always feel an undercurrent of anxiety. But the more we exercise human sensitivity and intelligence, the stronger and more harmonious our society can become, because we will have tapped into the truth that is here for everyone. Within this unity, we can appreciate the diversity of human systems, and our confidence and strength as a global community will grow.

When my father talked about *creating* enlightened society, he envisioned all individuals being introduced to their basic goodness because, being individual, we are part of society. We got here through a mother and a father, and the world we came into is the product of many minds and hands. Since technology has made our society global, it is more important than ever to understand that the individual is part of a whole, and therefore each of us is responsible for the future.

At this time, materialism and its consumeristic influence over every aspect of our lives is an invisible totalitarian regime. However, unlike previous totalitarian regimes, this regime is omnipresent, and we are all participating. If we think it's impossible to create enlightened society, that's a sign we've been so thoroughly convinced by this system that we can no longer visualize an alternative. Our minds have grown small with fixation on consumption as a means to satisfaction. In the past, monumental events, like the birth of Jesus and the rise of Christianity, the French Revolution and the rise of democracy, and, in our own time, 9/11, have woken us up and shifted our view of reality, shaking us from our collective cocoon into a wider space. In the future, Mother Earth herself might offer some natural occurrence that vaults us out of our fixation on materialism and individualism and into a more socially holistic understanding. This will send us digging deeply and reassessing our part in the current regime. Whether or not such an event occurs, now is the time to create enlightened society.

Let us mobilize ourselves on this natural path of collective transformation. As we reawaken our strength and bring enlightened society into existence, we will enter a new dimension of spiritual revolution where we regard human society as the living and breathing being it has always been. We have entered a time when spirituality no longer means simply individual liberation—nor would that be possible, given our global connectivity. But it is up to each of us as individuals to reinvigorate our sense of worthiness and be here for the planet. That is how we will have the bravery to touch the future in each moment.

The point of this global self-reflection is to open our eyes to our own vision. Once we have confidence in the basic nature of things, we are more immediate in our life. The word *forward* is conventionally understood to mean

"onward, so as to make progress toward a successful conclusion." *Forward* can also mean "toward the future." Thus
it is linked with the word *continuous*, meaning that when
we have this kind of vision, the continuity of our intention is not severed.

When I asked my father, "Will society ever be enlightened?" I was asking a cosmic question with a cosmic
doubt. When my father said, "That's not really the point,"
I realized that he was helping to counter that doubt. My
question was handicapping all humanity. It should have
been, "When is enlightened society not possible?"

With this question, I can see my father smiling and
answering, "That's the point."

5

CHAOS IS GOOD NEWS

I ASKED MY father, "If everything is basic goodness, why is life so confusing?" It seemed to me that the world was becoming ever more crowded, speedy, anxious, and intense. People were acting less compassionate, more aggressive, and more prideful. Society seemed painful, competitive, and confused. What if we all became so isolated and scared that we forgot to take care of one another?

Knowing this was in my heart, my father said that pain comes from people and society not recognizing their own wakeful potential. When people are not being genuine to themselves, they experience suffering. Then he said something that I think he meant to be consoling, but the statement puzzled me: "Chaos is good news."

"What could possibly be good about chaos?" I replied.

My father went on to explain that he was referring to chaos in the way that the Greeks had used the word—to indicate a wide-open expanse. Chaos is the great space of emptiness that occurs before genesis. It is the openness where things fall apart and new creations arise. When you nearly crash your car or slip and nearly fall, your conceptual mind loses its grip and you are left in an open space. This space provides an opportunity to reconnect with what lies under the chaos and negativity—inherent awakened nature.

Another way chaos is good news is that when things seem very bad, there is a big opportunity for something good to take place. It is only through looking at what is going wrong that we will find out how to do things right. Recognizing chaos is actually the pivot point for touching our goodness, for it is not only an ultimate principle, without beginning or end, it is also a relative principle that works through the laws of nature. Spring becomes summer; autumn leaves fall down. Those natural laws are grounded in cause and effect.

I believe that the pain and confusion of the world is now so vivid and unavoidable that we have no choice but to acknowledge it. Perhaps this means that when we are finally fed up with torturing ourselves, others, and the planet, out of our exhaustion will arise a gap in which we come to our senses and collectively rediscover a more natural state. Only by staring directly at the confusion—examining it and absorbing its reality—will our species discover a way forward.

The point at which we fully comprehend the problem is the point at which the solution dawns. To enlighten means to "fully illuminate." We see the problem and find a solution. In this way, being unaware of the problem is not being enlightened, but being ignorant. Even on a personal level, when we have predicaments in our life, the answer is already there; we just need to be open to it. If we are tired, we need to rest. If we are overeating, we need to stop. In terms of enlightenment, the answer lies in our confidence in goodness.

Particularly in the West, when I propose the Shambhala principle of basic goodness and how it could be the foundation of an enlightened society, people think it is impossible. Yet it is the human vocation to make the impossible possible. As a species, even our existence is in many ways an impossibility. Scientifically, we are the most underequipped and vulnerable. We have no claws or fur. We are not that strong or fast.

What has allowed humanity to survive is our adaptability, which is rooted in society—the communication and exchange between individuals. As a species, our ability to adapt—"to join or fit into"—is totally based on doing what we humans do most successfully: create social harmony through our relationships. People working together has enabled our species to make the impossible possible.

During his worldwide travels, when he was in the Galápagos Islands, Charles Darwin formulated his theory about the success of a species. This theory of natural selection states that the most successful organisms are those that can best adapt to their environment. When a species does not adapt to its environment, it is out of tune with reality. Therefore, it is unable to succeed. Darwin's theory has been called "survival of the fittest," "survival of the aggressive," or "survival of the selfish."

In terms of our species, I prefer to look at the idea of natural selection as "survival of the good." I call it "the goodness factor." What has given us the upper hand in nature is our ability to organize and work together by observing, listening, compromising, caring, and responding appropriately. We express thought, communicate, and take care of one another. Our species' intelligence and flexibility have carried us this far in time. In this light, it is human nature to be in harmony with one another and the environment, and our survival depends on it.

As I've said before, aggression is the result of selfishness and fear, which shrink our perspective. Aggression surfaces at the point where we appear to make short-term gains, but we weaken our chances of survival in the long run, for as aggression consumes us, our perspective continues to shrink; we become rigid and lose our flexibility.

Our hearts harden. It becomes more difficult for us to make rational or conscious decisions, and we are hardly able to adapt because our view is so narrow that we can see only one possible solution to a problem—aggression. Aggression is a sign not of strength, but of fear, failure, and weakness. It means that all other possible avenues— compassion, kindness, and bravery—have failed.

Thus, it is dangerous to equate the survival of the fittest with the survival of the aggressive. As complicated and diverse as the world is, one of humanity's essential qualities is strength, and someone who has realized the nature of his or her true mind has the strength to be forceful when necessary—and also compassionate, loving, and kind. Compassion is a long-range solution that has a positive influence on our society and our economy. It stabilizes our lives and the lives of others. If our energy were simply aggressive, it would be too myopic and weak to have gotten us this far.

Yet at this intersection of the rise of technology and science, the fall of ethical standards, and economic and ecological instability, there is a danger—even with the concerted efforts of individuals and organizations to make the world a better place—that the habit of aggression will become stronger than the habit of compassion. Particularly since the Industrial Revolution, we have had greater means to oppose nature, taking advantage of the environment for our own gain. Through this greed and discontent we are consuming our planet and the natural resources it provides. The result is personal, social, and environmental deforestation. Many of us are already passionately involved in responding to this crisis because we know that Mother Nature has been at the survival game longer than we have and has more patience. If we do not create harmony among ourselves and the environment, if Darwin's theory is correct, eventually the elements will beat us.

It is true that climate change and economic instability are big practical issues. However, any long-term solution to our concerns is rooted in a deep psychic shift. When I would ask my father if enlightenment is possible, he would say, "Yes, because we have enlightened genes." In this time of chaos, if we can choose compassion instead of aggression, we will regain our connection to nature, and humanity could be here for many eons into the future, having created a society that works in partnership with the earth—by embracing our own enlightened qualities. How do we accomplish this practice? By being here now. When a great wind blows, we are immediately blown into the present moment.

In Shambhala, goodness is not only communication between humans; it is also communication with the elements and all living beings. This is known as *drala*, the natural communication that is always happening in our environment. The tides changing, the birds singing, and people kissing are living signs of the innate wish to communicate that percolates in all relationship. It is this warmth that binds us. The dance between the elements and our perceptions is a dance between the masculine and feminine principles: Our senses are always engaging with our environment. This, too, is enlightened society—the pure, clean communication of the living world.

At this critical juncture, if we second-guess ourselves and doubt our basic goodness—and the possibility of a society fueled by care and kindness—then we are reneging on our heredity. Defaulting to insecurity and aggression, not fully believing in our own compassion, is the opposite of bravery. If this cowardly state of mind begins to consume humanity, it is unlikely that we will create harmony with our environment and survive.

When my father expressed the notion that chaos is good news, he was highlighting the possibility that this age of confusion and turmoil offers humanity an unprecedented opportunity to be heroic in our daily lives. When things come to a head, there is an opportunity for change to occur. But we have to be ready for that opportunity. We can't just wait and think somebody else is going to do it.

Modern chaos theory posits that even a small change can dramatically shift the long-term behavior of a system. One thought, one word, one person can make a difference. Rather than feeling overwhelmed, deflated, and defeated, we can be proactive in the midst of chaos by paying attention. Many people are already cultivating this habit through the practice of meditation. Because we are able to access our own consciousness, with mindfulness—the ability to appreciate our own lives, moment to moment—we can see the connection between humans and the environment, and therefore nature itself. Then we can illuminate the confusion by reflecting on our presence here on earth.

Can we feel comfortable in our own minds and hearts? Compassion is not simply a feeble response to hard times. It is choosing not to pollute our own thoughts and our planet with the energy of aggression. Every morning, we need to contemplate what we're doing in our life today and how we will grow by connecting with those around us.

What are the signs of progress? Our body, speech, and mind become more gentle. At times we are able to bear difficulty without complaint. We might even begin to welcome chaos as an opportunity to engage in patience, generosity, discipline, meditation, exertion, and their binding factor, prajna—wisdom rooted in seeing things as they are. When we consider chaos good news, whatever comes our way—good or bad—has less power to obstruct our journey.

6

BEING BRAVE

A TIBETAN PROVERB says that when difficult situations arise, the good become better and the bad become
worse. When we don't trust our nature, challenging situations just feed our fear and doubt. Fear arises from a
lack of knowledge. Because we do not know our goodness, we have trepidation and insecurity. That puts us in
a self-protective mode. With such a limited view, we are
worriers, not warriors.

The strange thing about worry is that it actually does
not help. It compounds the situation, because our mind
is too contorted to feel what is happening. It is hard to
be present and confident because we are living in the future or the past instead of the present, which only spawns

more fear and worry. This is how the mind can be used as a weapon against humanity. However, when we feel our goodness, we become alert and caring, which takes us beyond hesitation about expressing our goodness. I call this "being brave."

Bravery is the key instruction within the Shambhala teachings. It means to embody the true nature of humanity, both personally and socially, with courage and insight. In short, it means to do the right thing. My father called it "living in the challenge." It is challenging times like ours that make us more interesting people. But to live in the challenge, we need a game plan that's not based in shallow inspiration or lukewarm conviction. It must have genuineness that stems from deep internal wisdom that is constantly radiating forth.

These days, challenges come in two spheres: external and internal. Externally, we are challenged by poverty, wars, famines, pollution, and climate change, caused, in large part, by systemic failures of our society to take responsibility for the planet. Internally, we are challenged by our doubt about our nature, by complex ethical questions, and by a mental culture of speed and aggression that overwhelms us with information, possibilities, and distractions. It is easy to see how the external world influences the internal world, and how the internal reality affects the environment. In creating enlightened society, we must work within both spheres.

As I have already said, the cosmic mirror of basic goodness contains all of human society—doubt and confidence, confusion and liberation, warriors and cowards. According to the Shambhala treasure teachings, the cowards, who arose out of doubt, hid themselves in the jungles of negativity and acted like wild animals, churning up hatred, lust, and laziness. The warriors, who arose out of confidence, went to beautiful places and with love and generosity worked together to erect crystal palaces and sow fields of grain.

Obviously, we are not all only warriors or only cowards. At times in our lives, and even in the course of a day, we are brave, and at other times we are a little cowardly. Sometimes we are thoroughly engaged, embracing life with our very best qualities, and at others we are slacking off, indulging in the worst. How do we move our mind away from cowardice and toward bravery? My father said that to nurture bravery, first I should put my fearful mind into "the cradle of loving-kindness." When the mind is present in a healthy state, it feels good. That's why meditation has been proven to reduce stress: We are cultivating an environment of gentleness for the mind. With gentleness, the mind can sustain itself, and we become confident in our goodness.

Next, he said, I should uplift my behavior by knowing what to choose and what to discard. Life comes down to habit, which is what the mind holds on to. It can be a positive or a negative. The mind is always holding something, but certain thoughts or objects are more helpful than others because they lead to enlightenment instead of ego, aggression, or laziness. He told me to be a warrior on my own two feet.

Next he said I should develop equanimity. The weather changes all the time, and if my mind were to change with it, I could never be a warrior. Connecting with a bigger mind would take me beyond concepts like hope and fear, which he called "the trap of doubt." In the space of impartial mind, I could be playful and simple. Whether it's a good day or a bad day, goodness is our ground—as we cry and as we laugh. That is being brave.

Negativity is hesitation and doubt: small mind cluttering the space of big mind. It's easy to mistake it for how things really are. Jealousy, blame, complaint, ambition, fear—we take these as our view, until we remember they're just part of the bigger picture. With intelligence and confidence, we can connect with that moment of discovery and cultivate its potential by relaxing into big mind.

True relaxation suggests a deep underlying confidence in our enlightened nature. We do not have to manipulate, because we trust who we are. In an argument with a coworker, instead of trying to outwit him or her, we use our energy to connect to a bigger view—such as generosity, kindness, and other principles that we are engendering.

This allows us to maintain confidence in the inherent goodness in the situation.

When we practice like this, we see that sadness and joy are two sides of the same coin. In any situation, we can doubt our enlightenment, which makes our mind smaller and more fixed. Anger, impatience, and anxiety—all are telltale signs that we're slipping from the view of big mind. We feel the need to convince, complain, and cajole. Must we always get the last word in? This brings tears. Or we can have confidence in our enlightenment, which expands our mind and keeps it flexible. This brings joy.

A mind relaxed enough to trust the boundlessness of its inherent wisdom and compassion is no longer fooled into thinking that getting the best seat at the concert, winning every argument, or finding faults in others is going to bring happiness. With equanimity, we can laugh at how hard we try to hold on to our speed and hassle. When we encounter another person, we can let our nature shine through. Instead of crying and complaining, we can laugh and offer kind words. We do not have to tell half-truths to build confidence, because we have confidence in the whole truth. Our eyes are opening to the myriad ways that inherent joy and enlightenment are here.

In these essential instructions, my father was showing me how to connect with windhorse, the element that brings success. Windhorse represents the joy of being free of a mind that is fixated on passion and aggression as a

way to realize our ambitions. Its legs represent dedication, thoughtfulness, exertion, and investigation. On its
back it carries the jewel of enlightenment. The energy of
windhorse is completely interdependent with living in the
challenge, for it connects us with unwaning and authentic
bravery.

The Shambhala tradition regards any aspect of life—
family, work, friends, solitude—as an avenue for this kind
of bravery. When we see each day as the path of awakening to goodness, everything we meet is an opportunity
to choose confidence over doubt. However, if we use our
activities as a buffer against moving forward, those same
activities become a nesting ground for cowardly traits—
elements of deception that keep us from being fully present. In that case, we are hiding from our own bravery.

One characteristic of hiding is that we are always
self-observing. Self-observing comes from not trusting
our nature and therefore keeping the reins tight on our
mind. It is different from self-reflection. When we are
self-reflecting, we are relaxing the mind and opening to
goodness in the present moment by extending our senses.
When we are self-observing, we are tightening the mind
and hiding in a closed system bounded by hesitation and
limited concepts about who we are in the world. Socially
we are threatened; thus we lack vision and fear change.

Because we are hiding, and therefore sheepish in
our mental and physical behavior, it is hard to embody

goodness. Not being present creates private havens for many of our setting-sun habits. We hunch when we drink our coffee. We are unable to look our spouse in the eye. We fidget as we meditate. We pursue entertainment. We actually feel comforted by the lack of synchronicity between our thoughts and our actions. When we do experience something wholly and completely, it is disconcerting and disorienting. Our lack of bravery becomes a magnet for negativity, attracting like-minded individuals.

There is nothing like success, whether it is big or small, so if you care to move forward in your life by being present, you should begin by looking at the conditions of your life. In your daily cycle, where are you placing your mind? What environmental influences are you encouraging?

A warrior with confidence has an air of splendidness that comes from not hiding anywhere. Lightening up our habits by no longer hiding in them allows us to shine. My father called this glow *ziji*, which means "brilliant, radiant confidence." He decided to use the word *confidence* because it describes a nonconceptual feeling, neither spiritual nor worldly—the radiance that arises when we are brave. Such confidence leads to what Plato refers to as "virtue." The word *virtue* is rooted in the Latin *vir*, which means "humanity." Aristotle speaks of virtue as "the manifestation of the good."

When students asked the Buddha, "How should I practice?" the Buddha would answer, "Bring virtue to whatever you are doing. When you sew, make garments with the thought of compassion. When you cook, make food with patience. When you play music, offer it with generosity. Let whatever you are doing become your meditation, and your path will deepen." These days we call this kind of activity "meditation in action."

One of the recommended ways to bring meditation into action is wholeheartedly embracing the path of virtue. How do we determine what is virtuous? We look at the result. Being mindful, feeling compassion, and exercising patience lead to pleasure and lightness of mind. Being angry, jealous, or proud leads to pain because it constricts the mind and makes our consciousness thicker. We take charge of our life by knowing which qualities we want to enhance.

There will always be hardened hearts and mental anomalies—depression, anxiety, and fear—just as there will always be behavioral anomalies and environmental anomalies. From the perspective of bravery, these conditions are not the norm, and when they arise, they should be treated with compassion and concern. That's how a fearful mind becomes a joyful mind. In order to be brave, we must trust that underneath it all, there is sanity and openness.

It is critical to understand that there is a direct relationship between our internal ethics and the external environment. For example, at this time, people are using

more and more pharmaceutical drugs, mainly to counteract two states of mind—elation and depression. The
need for so many drugs clearly indicates that individually and collectively our minds are feeling the pressure of
life's challenges. Essentially, we are either too tight or too
loose. If, in our confusion, we begin to consider the extreme states of depression and elation to be normal—no
longer believing the mind capable of sustaining its own
strength and balance—at that point, we will have reneged
on being brave in relationship to our mind. We will have
given up on our sanity.

If we give up on our ability to hold a balanced view,
we will create an air of defeatism, psychically and envi-
ronmentally. Considering these external challenges in-
surmountable, human dignity will become even more
degraded, and we will finally be completely subscribed to
the belief that the nature of humanity is vile behavior,
cruelty, and lack of purpose. Kindness, appreciation, and
decency will be relics from a bygone era. We will destroy
our planet and extinguish the brilliance of our own species, which is defined by its success against seemingly in-
surmountable odds. Therefore, it is important to come out
of hiding and be brave. Being brave comes from training
and intelligence. We must be versatile, imaginative—even
clever—relating with dignity and purpose to the earth,
not cowering from our responsibility to protect it. In order
to create enlightened society, humanity must rediscover

its bravery. We can each start where we are by looking directly at our mind and how we live our life. Are we rousing our confidence to create good human society? What prevents us from stepping beyond fear and habit? If we all nourish our bravery, we can help shift society toward goodness.

At this critical point, can humanity be brave? Warriors must have tactics; we cannot just run headlong into battle and hope for the best. Internally, we need to probe the depths of kindness, patience, intelligence, love, and respect in order to free these qualities and restore balance to society, which in turn will lead to more balance in the environment. How can we build an economy that does not promote environmental destruction or social imbalance, from which arises warfare? Can we relate to one another in a genuine and respectful way?

Before my father left Tibet, his own teacher gave him final words of wisdom. He said, "Help them be decent people." Being decent comes down to being brave. We appreciate life and everything in it, and we are not afraid of our own brilliance and creativity. Let us stand on the ground of goodness and care. This is bravery: using the challenge of daily life to sharpen our mind and open our heart.

Part II

FEELING

7

KINDNESS IS THE UNIVERSAL EXPRESSION

AFTER I HAD been empowered as the future sakyong, my father shared some more essential instructions. He said, "Be kind." Then he gave me a big hug, and expressed how much he loved me. This was both a verbal and emotional transmission. He was saying to be kind, and through his physical gesture, he was also transmitting kindness, empathy, love, and gentleness, the enlightened qualities he wanted me to embody.

Through my father's instruction, I began to see that kindness is more than a randomly experienced emotion, more than simply a social nicety. With the word *kind*, my father was pointing to an invisible highway of human connectivity that is paved by our longing to communicate.

In this light, *kind* stems from *kin*, or "family." We are related through our kindness. It is empathy, the ability to feel what others feel. This is how we exchange with one another and the environment.

My father, like many loving parents, would hold my hand in times of difficulty and challenge. He was teaching me to feel, showing me how just being with someone else is a powerful method of engendering kindness. That human contact allowed me to relax and feel my own strength and potential, opening my heart and letting its natural kindness flow forth.

Ironically, in our speedy lifestyle, it is easy to forget to be kind even to ourselves. The emphasis on fulfilling our personal desires begins to overshadow the greater need to connect. We all have our dreams to fulfill, but in order to really fulfill them, we must realize that we are dependent on one another. Simply by having been born human, we are naturally part of society. Naturally, by being human, we are social creatures.

One of the key elements in being kind is gentleness. Gentleness is nonaggression. The aggressive mind has a hard time being present, because it wants something else to be happening. Therefore it is always trying to manipulate or create a situation, and the tension of that self-involved struggle suppresses our ability to connect with the environment. If we can't be where we are, we can't feel. If we can't feel, we are unable to appreciate and care, and our most human trait—the yearning to connect—is confined. We are like a river that is meant to flow but has now been dammed.

Although kindness is invisible, we know when it is present and when it is not. A society without high regard for simple human feelings is in jeopardy. Families dissolve when members are not willing to be kind, and children lack role models. Many may feel that kindness is impractical: It doesn't get us what we want; we have no time for it, or we have more important things to do. However, kindness is extremely practical, for it cuts through isolation, fear, and aggression. All of us can remember moments of kindness that changed our day, at least—and maybe our lives. When we relegate kindness to mere social courtesy, we are handicapping our access to the ambassador of love and compassion—deeply held powers of the human heart. If we want to continue to evolve, we should cultivate ordinary kindness. With kindness, we will shift our future.

Human happiness is based not just upon individual gratification; the happiness of humans is directly associated with the ability to share. Often we are told that if we buy certain products, we will be happy; but if we are sitting by ourselves trying to enjoy our purchase, we are missing the essential ingredient. The reason we enjoy sharing and exchanging is their intimate connection to kindness and friendship. If humanity were not rooted in some fundamental healthiness, the innate desire to communicate would not be so linked with our own happiness—and thus, to our own survival. Enlightened society is like a communal heart that pulsates with kindness in order to keep us all connected.

If we cannot be kind to one another, clearly we have lost touch with our own humanity. I feel that the increasing isolation, fear, and aggression in our world is a sign that we are struggling with this very point. At times, it seems that anger has become our most valid form of communication: When people are expressing anger, they are said to be expressing their true feelings. Such anger is often really frustration that we have not allowed ourselves to feel, or fear that our future is less than bright. It is also our frustration at having created a society that lacks the communal openness in which kindness and gentleness are the preferable responses. As a result, our natural tendencies are being stifled. If we regard anger as the most acceptable expression, we have reduced all the ways we could communicate down to this single method. While anger can acknowledge the problem, anger itself cannot solve the problem.

In order to solve our human problems, we must rely on a variety of methods. Our nature is to understand through empathy all the conditions and complications that human beings face. Out of that comes kindness, because in order to solve any problem, we need to understand the problem, and in order to understand, we need the open interchange of two-way communication. Kindness gives us the feeling that we *do* belong—and that we can make a difference in how history unfolds.

Even though we live in a time when science and practicality dominate, if we want to be happy and successful, we must rely on human qualities as well. Kindness is not necessarily as strong as love, which is deeper, or as distant as pity, where we might hold ourselves above another, and that is its power: Kindness is easy to integrate into our day-to-day exchanges with others. As we walk, talk, eat, work, and feel, we can keep the kindness flowing. It doesn't have to be a heroic task. It can be as simple as letting go of our agenda for a moment to open the door for somebody, inquire about another's family, take time off from work to celebrate progress or a birthday, or to look at coworkers and, instead of secretly wishing for their demise, know that just like us, they want to be treated kindly.

When someone's got your number and they're calling it a lot, kindness isn't always easy. How do we encourage kindness? We need to make time for self-reflection and cultivate that time into a habit. This is a space in the day when we examine our view. What is our motivation? We may feel inspired by the Dalai Lama, Aung San Suu Kyi, Nelson Mandela, or others who exemplify kindness and compassion. How do we follow their example? That is our self-reflection. We begin by looking in our own being for the qualities we admire, and contemplating them. Then we reenter our day and try to use them whenever we can. Look for the motivation, contemplate it, and act on it.

Self-reflection is not something we do just once in order to solve our problems. We need to do it consistently, like drinking water and eating food. Just as we spend a portion of each day making our bodies clean and strong, we need to have a daily cycle of self-reflection to stabilize our motivation. Without that, it will sway like a tree in the wind of thoughts passing through. Acting mindlessly on those swaying thoughts, we can easily pollute any situation. When someone acts aggressively, our own aggression rises, and then we've only increased the conflict in the world, instead of reducing it with kindness.

We have to be able to see what is genuine. In the process of reflection, we are unearthing our treasure, and testing our basic goodness over and over again. That is the meaning of warriorship. What is our attitude altogether? What is our motivation? It is to tap into the goodness in ourselves and illuminate the day, seeing the world through the eyes of a warrior. That is confidence.

A key aspect of warriorship is having vulnerability and trust. Vulnerability is being open to the goodness within us and others. Trust is understanding what we are doing and why we are doing it. Without vulnerability and trust, we are perpetually dragged down to the lower realms of existence: Our minds are reduced to fraternizing with aggression, attachment, and pride. Because we are not rising to our potential, we act in cowardly ways.

Possibly our minds are strong enough to see that everyone is in the same boat. We all have the same hopes and dreams, as well as the same obstacles. Suffering and pain arise because we think we're separate. Kindness teaches us that we aren't separate from others at all: They are having the same experiences we are, because all beings want happiness, and no being wishes to suffer. Being kind is a simple practice, but it is also a transforming practice, because as we continue, the conceptual boundary between "us" and "them" begins to melt. That is how we create an environment that expresses lightness and humor, with an appreciation of life and the goodness of who we are. Those are the building blocks of an enlightened society.

When my father said on that day that I should be kind, he was pointing to the truth that engaging in this trait is what makes us human. When we are kind, we are looking at one another as brethren. Even though we may not trust it or believe it, just being with that possibility has an impact on what we say and do, and how we move forward.

Let us cultivate a culture of kindness. In that moment, we are determining the outcome of the world.

8

LIFE IS A CEREMONY

EVERY SUMMER, MY father and I would go into the mountains, pitch tents, and conduct a meditation program for a hundred people or so. This gathering would last for about ten days, with all of us living in tents arranged in a large square. I could tell that my father enjoyed it a great deal, for to some degree he had grown up in such surroundings. In the nomadic culture of Tibet, large caravans would move from one location to another and pitch tents, creating small communities out of nothing.

I always looked forward to these gatherings outdoors in the fresh air. At the end of the program, I would feel sad because when we packed up the tents, our city would disappear. At that point, indoor living had no appeal for me. Once I asked my father, "What do we do now?" He replied, "Life is a ceremony."

He meant that through our view, contemplation, and activity, every day we are transforming commonly held internal principles into an external social reality. In our summer encampment, with our meals, our practice, and our songs, we were transforming the principle of basic goodness into an enlightened society. All actions in life are done with some intention. What is the basis of that intention? For the warrior it is always to engage in an activity with confidence in goodness.

The power of ceremony is that through the rituals of our day, we understand who we are. In details such as what food we eat or how we use our time, we are creating self-identity and establishing value systems. However, the root principles of any particular social ceremony may not necessarily be conscious, or even understood, by the members of the society. Therefore it is important to examine the underlying assumptions that guide our social ceremonies—and to explore whether these principles are natural, genuine, and good. What are our ceremonies celebrating? We may discover that the status quo that we believe to be reality was in fact created by somebody else's game plan.

The shared ceremony of society creates the layout and design of everything from homes and businesses to cities and countries. It celebrates our collective values and priorities, which we are always projecting onto the blank canvas of space and time. There is a New York ceremony, an Amsterdam ceremony, and a Beijing ceremony.

Over the centuries, we humans have held different principles about how reality should be celebrated, reflected by the particular environment. In ancient Greece, life was a ceremony of relating to the gods, who represented forces such as war and wisdom, power and love. Large and intricate temples were built as houses for the gods and their human conduits. They also served as monuments to the ceremony of civic pride, conveying through their form the values of balance and harmony. Later, with the rise of Christianity, churches dominated the landscape, adapting the structure of the Roman civic basilica—which was conveniently shaped in the form of a cross—into the house of a single god. With the rise of humanism, the ceremony centered around philosophy and art, and the architecture melded classical concepts with evolving standards of beauty that communicated humanity as the center of the natural world. In the modern era, where materialism and commercialism dominate, skyscrapers identify our cities, their shiny minimalist forms reflecting the flat, superficial, and power-seeking ceremony of our age. What are we celebrating?

When a group of individuals decides what is real, and then bring that decision into a collective ceremony, this becomes social reality, shaping our homes, our workplaces, our towns, cities, and nations. It is based not just upon any single individual's concept, but on a collective agreement anchored in the relationship between beliefs and daily actions.

A good example of this is our modern calendar. In general, the modern calendar is organized into five days of work and two days of rest. In some cultures, those days of rest are divided into one day for the family and one day for religion. However, as materialism takes over and family and religion become less important, the two days of rest are more likely to be allocated to shopping, entertainment, or more work. Thus, in our current ceremony, humanity spends most of its time making things and buying things. Within this system, personal growth and spirituality are not priorities, because there is little room left in the calendar for examining the purpose of life and developing one's heart and mind.

My father would always say, "Desire leads to more desire, it does not lead to satisfaction." What leads to satisfaction is appreciation. That comes from paying attention. However, our modern ceremony is colored by speed, and desire crowds out the time and space to appreciate. We rarely feel satisfied, and therefore we never get what we want, because we are unable to be present. We slowly build up a level of resentment and aggression because innately the human mind needs periods of satisfaction daily, which are available only in the present moment. Even if it is only finding time to take a shower or to feel good that we made it to work after missing the bus, we need to find small victories in the day—and slow down enough to appreciate them.

Ironically, the ultimate purpose of buying and selling is to be happy, but if the more we buy and sell, the less happy we are, we see that we are living a mistake. We are empowering the larger forces of others' ceremonies over ours—be they advertisers, retailers, banks, or other corporations—an approach that influences our life and society. Caught in the cycle of craving and fixating, we rarely question the purpose of our silent participation in this ceremony. Our world of desire and consumerism seems to drive itself along, as if propelled by some invisible force. As I meet leaders in my travels, I see that even at the very top, people are wondering who is in charge. It is as if humanity's destiny were a giant rudderless ship that is drifting out to sea. Whose ceremony is this? What is our intention, and where is it leading us?

We are all here on earth to see what we can offer, as opposed to what we can take. A life based upon what we can take leads to a society where the only barometer of success is the accumulation of material goods. We want to be happy, we want to have purpose, but we are spinning out in an attempt to find it in something outside ourselves. All this leads to suffering.

Throughout history, spiritual groups have retreated

from the conventional ceremony of daily life in order to create their own ceremony within the ceremony. They have reduced their worldly activities in order to turn inward. Therefore, the spiritual began to represent a separate set of values because it was identified with people who had rejected worldly values. However, the Shambhala principle advocates that spiritual and worldly values are not separate. What makes them seem separate is that our intention in satisfying worldly values is often driven by unsavory emotions such as ambition and envy. When my father said, "Life is a ceremony," he was using the word *ceremony* to convey that we can arrange our everyday life to reflect and generate our understanding of deep and transcendent principles.

I know through my training that individuals can arrange their lives as ceremonies of goodness. Through the power of the intention within the ceremony, enlightenment can occur. Let me illustrate this. In the tradition of tantra and esoteric Buddhism, a traditional component of one's daily ceremony is called *sadhana*, a Sanskrit word meaning "great accomplishment." Through certain rituals one establishes a *mandala*, or "circle," of enlightened energy. Then one meditates according to the particular expression of that mandala—be it compassion, wisdom, or skillful means. It is a process of visualizing enlightened qualities, identifying with them, and radiating them out into the larger space. One is then more likely to embody those qualities in the ceremony of life.

Even as a young man, I had received transmissions from my father and other eminent teachers concerning the details of setting up a mandala and performing the ceremony of *sadhana*. But when we gathered every summer and pitched tents, my father was teaching me an even bigger lesson—that the kindness and compassion in the heart of humanity are natural, available in every activity. The words *spiritual* and *worldly* are simply conceptual delineations.

In any mandala, the reason we identify with enlightened energy is so that we can embody it in order to help others. At our encampment, we were creating the mandala of enlightened society, using our loyalty to goodness to create an atmosphere of possibility. I am defining *society* as the network between individuals. It has also been described as "a friendly association" because just as the nature of humanity is basic goodness, society's natural energy is care and kindness. From that, the ceremony of enlightened society arises. Society, from that point of view, is simply a mirror reflecting how many minds feel about themselves. A good society is a matter of individual minds self-empowering their instinctive goodness. This has a dramatic effect on the ceremony of life, exuding potency into all spheres of activity.

Naturally, associating with awake principles increases our chances of being awake ourselves. Remembering these principles becomes a natural antidote to any obstacles we face. Therefore, with this approach, we come in contact with a deeper purpose of life. Instead of just trying to get through the day, we actually gain and learn throughout the day. This attitude is the hallmark of a warrior, who knows that every day is an opportunity for freshness and discovery that will never happen again. As my father said, "Every day is a special day." Thinking that each day is just the same old day does not lead to awakening, but to habituation.

When we do not want to acknowledge each day as being special, the coward is arising. We want to retreat into our minds, and in particular into comforting, preexisting thoughts. Therefore, this notion of being a coward is not to be willing to face what is currently occurring, which is simply life. Often this stems from being very fixated on ourselves. Naturally, in order to live and regard each moment as special, we have to share—enjoying and celebrating with others, as well as helping them. Even in the Tibetan Buddhist tradition of remaining for years in solitary retreat, it is the mental comfort of extending love and compassion to all beings that allows powerful meditators to grow from training the mind. This notion of sharing frightens the coward but invigorates the warrior. If we don't orient our day toward spiritual growth, the speed of our life takes over, fueled by habitual patterns. Some habitual patterns are a source of inspiration; others just drain our energy.

We want to infuse our day with good habits, such as using patience instead of anger, so we can turn seemingly mundane situations into a ceremony of goodness. Such a ceremony begins with morning self-reflection—Which quality will I strengthen today?—and ends with an evening check-in—How do I feel about what happened? How can I move forward tomorrow?

Through a ceremony of goodness, we create steadiness and resolve—core qualities of a warrior. Once we have decided to be brave, we stay with it and keep challenging our boundaries by letting go of negative habitual patterns, such as complaining when we wish something were different. This leads to a sense of delight.

Recently I was reading the memoirs of Yung-lo, emperor of the Ming, who was a great warrior-bodhisattva king and patron of Tibetan Buddhism. It is amazing to see how early his day started, how late it went, and how he was there for every moment in a dedicated and exalted way. Whatever role we are in, we can follow his example and make steadiness and presence part of our ceremony.

The process of genuinely engaging in our ceremony has an outer level and an inner level. Fifty percent of the outer level is discipline—just showing up. Because of all the distractions and trauma in the world these days, it is getting harder to be there for the present moment. So often now our ceremony involves plotting an escape by contemplating something we'd rather be doing, the last thing we enjoyed doing, or the next thing we want to do. We would like to go to some cozy little place and just hope it all gets better. Whether it is showing up at work or showing up in an intimate relationship or a family, *how* we show up is important. Truly being there takes energy.

When we are fully engaged, we realize that there is no cozy little place as such—only confidence in our own goodness. To be brave is to be present. This is the inner aspect of practice. It's how we learn to draw power from our own strength. Sometimes it takes bravery even to get out of bed and face the day.

Now we must wake up and see that we are colluding in creating the current global ceremony—and that we have the power to change it. Fortunately, the die for human destiny has not been cast; however, we are in the process of casting it. The longer we participate in creating a monolithic ceremony of speed, desire, and discontentment, the more challenging it will be to awaken to our nature.

Of course, we have to discover for ourselves whether it is true that humans and their society are good. But if we're not buying into that reality, then we are buying into some other version—the reality of capitalism, materialism, or depression. In every present moment, we have the ability to create the reality of human goodness. We can use the Shambhala principle to take charge of our ceremony and bring the world into it.

How would your buying change if each time you made a purchase you did so with intentions of kindness, appreciation, love, and intelligence? How would your business operate if you applied the Shambhala principle to it? How would your education change if you embraced goodness, not pessimism, as your core outlook?

When our summer meditation encampment was ending, I always felt trepidation about going back into the world. I was experiencing the rub between two different ceremonies. Within the encampment, a ceremony based on community, discipline, and bravery was being encouraged. Once we reentered the more typical North American world, a ceremony based on individualism, speed, and consumerism was being extolled. After a few summers I began to realize that I had regarded the outside world as "normal" in the sense of "that's just how things are." But once I understood the notion of ceremony, I realized that what I was regarding as "normal" was just as much a ceremony as our encampment. What made the rituals of one ceremony more appealing than the other was that I had a greater affinity for the one ceremony's principles, and therefore I enjoyed it more. When my father told me that life is a ceremony, he was saying that the only reason I could not experience this goodness in the secular world was that I had disempowered it through the ceremony of nonawakening.

Thus, when we headed back into the everyday world, I realized that it was up to me to create my own ceremony. In buying into the current arrangement, I had disempowered my own feeling of goodness, so I was seeing the world as a closed system. However, it is inherently available to be empowered and arranged in an innumerable variety of ways. Now I knew that I preferred being awake to being asleep, and I understood why my father emphasized the need for discipline and structure at our summer encampment—insisting that we pay attention to how we dressed, how we spoke, what we did, and how we engaged with others. It was all part of creating an awake ceremony.

In reality, our planet is simply a small floating blue sphere in space. Our social reality is created by our ongoing ceremonies. Can we as a global community create the ceremony of basic goodness? Or will we continue to participate in a ceremony of social animosity that leads only to disempowering the human spirit?

9

JUST YOU AND ME

WHEN I WAS about fourteen, I asked my father how I would take my training forward. I expected him to tell me to do longer periods of deep meditation, or to study some profound texts of our tradition. Instead, he gave me a curious answer: "You should learn how to host a dinner and have conversation." When he answered my question in this surprising way, he was giving me another essential instruction. As a young boy, however, I thought, How could having polite dinner conversations be the culmination of my father's profound spiritual journey?

The next evening I sat down to have dinner with my father. I asked, "Is there anyone else?" He replied, "It's just you and me." When my father said, "Just you and me," he was communicating the essence of society. Beginning with the relationship between mother and child, the dynamic between two individuals is the source of secret and invisible power. Even though relationships between parents and children, or between romantic partners, can become confused, nonetheless the lineage of humanity stems from this caring feeling, the radiant hum of life. Society is based on the relationship between male and female, parent and child, friend and friend, customer and waitperson, boss and employee. Good human society comes about through strength in our interchanges with others.

Because of war and instability, we have been afraid to feel the basic goodness of society. However, it is always inherent—even in our society now. We can see this in an ordinary way: People follow laws, drive on the proper side of the road, and provide food and goods for others daily. We take responsibility for raising our children, regarding their education as important. Even in entertainment, we are not solely absorbed in tragedies, but innately wish for a happy ending. We naturally want something good to occur. This shows that society does not simply run on greed and aggression, but on an invisible network of love and goodwill. It is within this context that my father considered the simple act of sharing a meal and conversing to be the most advanced spiritual training. As we eat and talk, we relax our senses and touch the goodness that is omnipresent. This underlying force is the beating heart of humanity, and in this heart lies our future. What allows us to relax is our confidence in it.

When my father and I were having dinner, I realized that our emotions—my feeling of who I was, his feeling of who he was, and my feeling of who he thought he was and his of who he thought I was—were the threads in the fabric of our exchange. During the course of that dinner there were moments of silence, laughter, question-and-answer, conversation, simple exchange, long eye contact, smiles, frowns, and squints, as well as hand gestures. The glance of my eye, the tone of my voice, the thoughts arising in my mind were not inconsequential or minor; they were the very foundation of enlightened society.

By simply acknowledging my father, I was engendering respect. By hearing him, I was developing the ability to listen. By appreciating him, I was discovering kindness. By enjoying him enjoy his meal, I was discovering love. By not immediately coming to a conclusion about what he was saying and becoming upset that I did not agree, I was developing patience. By trying to see things from his point of view, I was developing understanding. By simply paying attention and being in the moment, I was developing mindfulness. By being curious, I was sharpening my intelligence. By listening to his stories and hearing what he had been through, I was using empathy to connect. By giving him my time, I was cultivating generosity. By appreciating the opportunity just to have this moment, I was feeling gratitude. By letting go of what I was planning to say next and listening to his words, I was experiencing selflessness. By realizing that not everything was going to go my way—and still attempting to direct the conversation and the evening—I was discovering passionlessness and letting go. By accommodating what was happening, I was learning acceptance. By realizing that I would never understand the totality of who my father was, I was appreciating mystery.

When my father said, "Just you and me," he was not implying that no one else wanted to come. Having three people would not weaken the dynamic of two people; the dynamic would be multiplied, since the exchanges would still be one to one. With more people, the *me* would still be *me*, and the *you* would revolve. At any given moment, you can make eye contact with only one person. You may, in rapid succession, engage with one person and then another, but just as your mouth can say only one word at a time, so your eyes can focus on only one person. Even in a large city, the relationships are still between two individuals.

As the evening progressed, my father and I both considered our exchange worthwhile—not simply idle or irritating. We were open to each other and paying attention. The care, curiosity, and kindness that naturally flowed between us were society itself, and our exchange was illuminating and expanding those qualities. By appreciating each other, we were appreciating humanity. All became one, and that one was basic goodness.

Society is made up of all of us playing "just you and me." We may know some people better than others, so we have more to say to them. But every relationship contains the seeds of society. If we do not develop the ability to exchange with another, our social skills diminish. However, "just you and me" is not about whether we like somebody or not. In reality, we often get along with someone one day but not the next. Inevitably, even with people we like, at some point we become impatient and fail to listen to them or respect them, and that relationship may dissolve. The point is to appreciate the act of exchanging with another. This is how we will bring an enlightened society into being. If we refrain from full engagement, we are weakening the network.

While our society of two was having dinner together, my father was teaching me that in that moment of just you and me, a culture was being developed. Whether these interactions bring cheerfulness or depression, whether we learn from them or not, they always play a role in forming who we think we are. Each one of us is our own culture. The importance of the person or the conversation—or even whether we can be fully present without wishing to rush off—doesn't matter so much: Our perception of ourselves is being formed by the exchange.

Beginning to see society as "just you and me" completely changes our relationship to others, because appreciating and respecting others in daily exchanges affects our relationship to our own self-identity and therefore to society as a whole. Often, because we doubt our own basic goodness, we cannot begin to fathom another's. But with this approach, a conversation between ourselves and another becomes an important social ceremony.

When my father and I sat by ourselves, it was a ceremony of enlightened society not necessarily because we had perfected every attribute, but because our mutual conviction in our essence had created an air of openness and generosity. As an enlightened warrior, he had established unequivocal faith in human nature, and his sheer conviction in this principle was all-pervasive. Even though my understanding and faith may not have been as strong, I had already established my own level of certainty. Although it was unspoken, all our interactions were highlighting this understanding. Our communication was not about the content of our conversation, nor was it the point of our conversation; rather, our communication was about an environment of deep respect for humanity—in particular, for the power of our minds.

Thus, the container of human interaction not only creates our self-identity, but also begins to form our opinion of the world. We are not two people separate from the world; our dialogue is creating the world. My father infused our relationship with his enlightened behavior and view, and the pathways of our interactions became paved with the Shambhala principle. While this was occurring, our self-identity as a twosome was being formed. The culture we were developing was based on our dyadic ceremony. Because we were mutually engaged in appreciation and respect, as we connected more deeply, our confidence in basic goodness expanded.

In both the Greek and Tibetan traditions, if there is respect and trust between teacher and student, their interaction can unlock the secrets of the universe. My father used to say that simply by thinking of his teacher Shechen Kongtrül, he could plug into a sense of very direct awareness. Likewise, marriage is a powerful relationship that can bring happiness and meaning. It creates family identity and family realities, which furthermore create cultures and tribes. In fact, for most humans, one good relationship with another person can be satisfying enough to provide meaning for a lifetime. Conversely, not having the opportunity to connect and converse with another can leave one feeling isolated and lost.

In our modern culture, who we are singularly seems to matter more than how we are communally. The power of one sometimes overshadows the power of two. Yet, for humans, being completely on one's own is unnatural. Simply by imagining human exchange, even in isolation, the mind grows. On the other hand, if we are living in a city full of people yet have no genuine exchange with others, we will experience a feeling of emotional poverty. Connectivity with others is how our species contextualizes and orients itself. We cannot underestimate the power of "just you and me." A world not valuing human interaction leaves many of us feeling isolated and alone. This naturally weakens any society and makes us vulnerable as a species.

Most of us do not consider a conversation with another as creating culture, or affecting the world much at all. Yet our seemingly minor exchanges have the power to gather momentum and begin to shift the social and environmental dynamics of our planet. The world is made up of millions and billions "just you and me" interactions, which include our relationship with everything—people, the environment, even our teacup. These interactions create energetic networks, expanding exponentially.

When my father said "Just you and me," he was highlighting this very point. In particular, he was saying that if I were to understand anything about society, it was important for me to know how to relate to the world in a dignified way. If—through misunderstanding, pride, or aggression—I somehow thought any exchange was inconsequential, by showing lack of respect, I demonstrated that I had clearly missed the point. By disempowering a simple exchange, I was disempowering myself.

When a society recognizes the importance of conversation, it is setting the stage for humanity's enlightened qualities to emerge. In particular, we are creating social vibrancy by honoring and respecting others' self-identity, which is reinforced by the exchange. By self-identity, I do not mean ego, but confidence in basic goodness. Ego is the basis of habitual patterns like fear and selfishness. The point of enlightened society is having the confidence to extend beyond those barriers. It is not just a spiritual egolessness; at the worldly level, too, we need egolessness. Otherwise, how are we to listen to each other?

A natural sense of curiosity and confidence arises as we begin to see that with the simplest daily interactions, we can create enlightened society—and that it takes only two to do it. Each interaction tests and hones our intellect and understanding, as well as our emotional flexibility. Such energy propels us toward success. Of course, for a society like this to occur, we need to have an underlying premise that human life is valuable, and that what we feel and think is worthwhile.

We may show respect for someone because he or she is famous, powerful, or wealthy; these are all valuable assets. However, if the power or wealth is gone tomorrow, we lose the basis of our exchange. When we base our interactions on the Shambhala principle, every person is worthy of respect. This principle also applies to global relations, which come down to the relationship between two diplomats. Lack of respect and appreciation creates a feeling

of hurt, which eventually leads to anger, and possibly revenge. Much global discord can be traced to a moment
when one person failed to appreciate and respect another.
When nations show lack of respect for each other, the
self-identity of each nation is threatened. If they appreciate this "just you and me" approach, we will have more
harmony.

In a society where the individual is exalted, it is harder
to tune into "you" because we are so involved with "me."
This isolationist policy makes it difficult to grow. Conversations become a one-way street instead of a two-way
rapport. On the other hand, in a society of "just you and
me," encounters become a way of celebrating our humanity because when we all contribute freshness and
flexibility to the one-to-one ceremony, our growth is exponential. Kindness and wisdom are displayed in many
directions. Ideas cross-pollinate; new theories arise. From
this self-invigoration, we create art, poetry, and literature,
as well as science and engineering. Let us now re-empower
the word *society* so that every time we have a conversation, it is an expression of possibility.

When my father said, "Just you and me," somehow I
knew that our ordinary exchange had implications for the
world. He was trying to communicate that if we two could
just be—be together, be relaxed, and be open—we would
create enlightened society. The occurrence of this simple

act would benefit everyone. Unlocking our own humanity would give humanity strength. Thus when I asked if anyone else was coming to dinner, and he answered, "Just you and me," he was really saying, "The whole world is coming to dinner."

10

WORKING FOR THE FUTURE

EVERY YEAR, MY father and I would celebrate the Tibetan New Year. Shambhala Day is a wonderful day when we rise early and raise a toast of Bombay gin to welcome the coming year. There are festivities all around, and the sakyong addresses the Shambhala community. In one of his last New Year's addresses, I remember my father dramatically proclaiming that we hold the threshold of the future in our hands. Building a good human society will take manual labor. It will not happen automatically.

This message struck me deeply. He was saying that we cannot rely on one or two people to suddenly move humanity in the right direction. We can't count on a magic spell being cast. Even finally discovering our worthiness does not particularly guarantee that a better society will materialize. Making good things happen still comes down to engaging ourselves thoroughly, with exertion. He said, "There will be no automatic big sweep." If the world is going to be a better place, it will take hard work.

Having engaged in the spiritual path, I personally know that progress happens only through hard work. Whether the path is worldly or spiritual, our success is directly related to effort and engagement. However, in spiritual work, people sometimes assume that positive developments will transpire spontaneously. For example, when Westerners were introduced to the Tibetan spiritual tradition with its many mystical elements, they assumed there must be some deep secret to moving forward on a spiritual path. The secret, as it turned out, was simply paying attention. My father often said that the magic occurs when we finally decide to appreciate each moment.

This simplicity and ruggedness were very much part of my father's character. He enjoyed hard work, and at the same time, there was magic. In that Shambhala Day address, he made another interesting comment: "When something bad is done, usually this is automatic." He was telling us again that making good things happen takes work. He said this is usually difficult because it goes against the grain of our habitual tendencies. As they say in golf, "If it feels wrong it's probably right." When something is good or virtuous, it is often very difficult. When things are contaminated or bad, they are often easy and seductive. We do not know what is good for us, and this confusion perpetuates the setting sun.

The Shambhala teachings of warriorship tell us that a good society is not based on a quick fix. A cruise ship does not turn on a dime, and good fortune must be earned. We may not always want to acknowledge it, but it is clear that to bring about any accomplishment there needs to be virtue, whether it's on a global, national, or an individual level. No matter how strong our leaders are, we must look at our own habits and begin to work with them. We can't hire out our own inner work, but we can do the manual labor with delight and decency.

In the Shambhala tradition, a time when humanity expects success and prosperity without working hard is known as a dark age. It is dark because our eyes are closed. When everything happens at the push of a button, we may be slow to realize that we have to work to wake up to our life. There is an interesting balance between enjoying the fruits of our labor and, at the same time, never forgetting that genuine happiness and joy come only through hard work. With so much automation happening, we could easily be fooled into thinking that creating a better world no longer requires us to fully engage. We think that things will also happen automatically in our internal world. Therefore, we fail to develop our positive qualities.

In reality, it is hard work to feel, appreciate, and

embody our nature, because in most cases that is neither our training nor our habit. If we become lazy or begin to fool ourselves into thinking that prosperity and happiness come with little effort, then collectively we have entered a slightly comatose state. We temporarily forget that a good human society requires work.

Before my father left Tibet, his teacher Shechen Kong-trül told him that when he found himself in the New World, he might discover that the people there would rather be asleep than awake. In many ways, our modern culture is a strange combination of speed and sleep. We forget that we are feeling creatures. We rush through traf-fic so we can get home to the comfort of our television. While this technology has the power to awaken empathy and thoughtfulness, the habit of using it as an escape dulls us to our own brilliance and tenderness.

What my father meant by "manual labor" is dedication—being thoughtful and investigating, rather than sinking into entertainment mode. When we exert our minds toward brilliance, we are simply using the laws of cause and effect to reveal sacredness as our collective reality. In particular, when we work hard to develop our own charac-ter and the character of our relationships, the fruits of our labor are personal and social durability and strength. We feel happier and more alive.

In fact, according to my father, when you achieve en-lightenment, you work even harder. If we work harder at awakening than we do at staying asleep, our exertion guarantees the future's success and durability. I myself would often wonder how working for the goodness of humanity could be anything but depressing or tiring, but when I asked my father how it felt to work so hard helping others, he said, "It is delightful."

Then I began to notice that by engaging in life with goodness, I was tapping into windhorse—an incredible reservoir of energy. Like a parent inspired by a child's potential, I discovered deep pools of discipline and generosity that brought cheerfulness and joy. Conversely, I discovered that when I became sucked into the quicksand of doubt and hesitation, a feeling of pain would occur, and I would lose energy. That's why helping others is delightful.

Thus, when my father proclaimed that we humans hold the threshold of the future in our hands, he meant that what happens next on earth is totally up to us. If we are willing to work for a wholesome future, then humanity's future truly does lie in our hands, for it will come about only through manual labor powered by our illumination. This creates a twinkle in the eye, brings a smile to the lips, and broadens our sense of conviction. In this light, humanity's future can occur because we are willing to hold it in our own hands.

CHEER YOURSELF UP

ONE MORNING, MY father asked if I was depressed. I told him I felt a little down. Somehow he could tell that I was waiting for him to give me some bit of inspirational wisdom. The instruction he offered was not what I'd expected. He looked at me and said, "Be where you are and who you are. That's how to cheer yourself up." Sometimes he would say, "Just do it." In this case, I must have looked puzzled, because he went on to explain that depression is the vanguard of obstacles and negativity, and that cheerfulness helps us guard against complication and adversity. In my life, his simple advice seems constantly to be proving itself true.

He might have said, "It's going to be okay," as parents

often do, but my father did not say it was going to be okay. In fact, he went on to say that right now the world is indeed depressed. On the surface many of us might think otherwise. Food and medicine are more widely available. As well, there are a number of stable governments. Technology makes it possible for millions of people to be connected. To say that the world is depressed seems contrary to how the world appears.

However, in using the word *depressed*, my father was not referring to the world's technological progress or apparent economic prowess. Rather, he was pointing to the depressed state of the human spirit. Despite the modern world's efficiency and industry, at an emotional level, the human spirit has been dampened, pressed down. It is at a low point, connected in particular to a habitual sense of inadequacy. We are in an age where depression arises from people feeling disempowered. There is a resolute feeling that the world may not in fact be all that good. With fundamental doubt about the purpose of our existence, an air of depression begins to suffocate all of us.

Naturally, when we feel that we are faulty, we mistreat ourselves, and then we mistreat others in the same way. When this lasts for a while, that depressed and aggressive state becomes the norm, and anything not depressing begins to appear naïve or unsophisticated. Even our nature appears insubstantial and small.

Thus, the psychic repercussions of materialism and

the ceremony of unworthiness have created a depressed culture, and the product of that culture is cynicism and doubt. Our sense perceptions are padded. Generally speaking, we are spooked by our own thoughts. Self-doubt arises, and we start doubting others. We forget about bravery as our minds are consumed by doubt, becoming unstable and fickle. Saying and doing negative things begins to make sense, and developing our warrior mind seems completely unrealistic. We have fallen into the cowardly realms, where the mind is trapped and depressed. It buys into aggression as a way to accomplish things. We have great confidence in anger, we are really certain that aggression is going to work, and we forget about patience and compassion—even toward ourselves.

The mind that arises from the combination of intelligence and a depressed state is essentially obsessed with negating everything, since the basic premise of such a mind is death and nihilism—hence my father's term, "the setting sun." To say our age is marked by setting-sun tendencies is not necessarily saying the world is over but that, as at the day's end, our care and curiosity are diminishing, like a clock winding down. There is a deflated feeling: Why work for the future when we feel that we are coming to the end?

Depression is a self-generated phenomenon for, conversely, when humanity is confident about its goodness, civilization takes on a natural glow. A sense of hope creates vision. Now, however, because we are living in a time of deep insecurity regarding the nature and purpose of being human, there is a chronic, gradual nullification of our spirit.

With his remark, my father was pointing out that human civilization seems to cycle through periods of depression and elation. From a meditative point of view, these two extreme states provide the main challenges to establishing mental peace and harmony. He said that during a depressed time, war is sometimes the way people and nations try to uplift themselves. It provides an economic stimulus and a purpose for living. The economy grows, and through anger or revenge, people's existence becomes vindicated. He called this a negative process of uplifting the human spirit, one in which we cheer ourselves up by creating enemies and destroying them.

Depression does not happen only at a national or economic level; it also occurs on a personal level. My father characterized this as the depression one feels when arising, or "early-morning depression." As soon as we wake up, we are caught in a dark cloud. It also has a quality of claustrophobia—we are comfortable within the small domain of limiting concepts. There is a feeling of finality. The day is over before it begins. This negative state of mind is not natural. In fact, it's continually created, and maintaining it is an exhausting process.

When we're depressed, we don't want to extend ourselves, so we become lazy. There's a low-grade anger involved. This very personal depression is poison for the human spirit. It leads to becoming further alienated from one's life and society altogether. That is why depression is equated with slow death. It is why our day becomes a constant vigil to avoid this feeling of depression. Because we feel deficient, we become depressed, and because we fear depression, we are desperate to alleviate it.

However, rather than connect with goodness, we often attempt to find a better feeling by immersing ourselves in entertainment, constantly waiting for the next issue of our favorite magazine or the next episode of our favorite television show. Ultimately we become seduced and sedated by entertainment because we think happiness lies in that direction. When we look to consumerism to cheer us up, our culture is happy to comply. In this light, the culture is in a speedy and heightened state of elation.

Elation is a sign that we are trying to appease our suffering by overstimulation. From travel to restaurants, coffee shops, and sports events, to endless online entertainment and shopping, we are blinded by the mirage that is trying to pretend depression does not exist. We are shopping and eating in an attempt to fill a void. However, on a subliminal level, these activities only feed our feeling of inadequacy.

Elation and depression are both signs of bewilderment, not knowing where to put our faith. We are investing in all kinds of things and coming up empty-handed. Our psychological state is completely related to the environment. When we feel inadequate, we consume the world around us rapaciously. In this vein, when my father was asked how we can help the environment, he would say the same thing, "We have to cheer ourselves up." This is the grassroots Shambhala approach to ecology—human beings cheering up, not by continuing to expend, but by connecting with their own dignity.

When my father said, "Cheer yourself up," initially it seemed almost naïve. I thought, Cheer myself up from what—and to where? When I thought further about his instruction, I began to realize that my doubt, with its accompanying critique, was not even really my own. My mind was cynical because I was already being consumed by the philosophy of depression. In this light, I began to wonder if in fact I had ever had a single original thought—one that was influenced by neither depression nor elation.

When I began to ponder more deeply, I wondered if I could produce even one thought that was completely free from the influence of Western or Eastern philosophy. I discovered that the opinions I was considering my own were usually a conglomeration of various philosophical worldviews and historical events, from the thoughts generated by the ancient Greeks, to the fall of God as the governing principle of humanity, to the First and Second World Wars.

Throughout this historical trajectory there have been periods of elation and depression. The natural tendency after depression is elation. Elation does not come about through the elimination of depression; rather, elation is the fear of depression. Let me explain. As opposed to the sinking feeling of depression, in elation our mind is high, fueled by the pursuit of happiness. We could even become elated about basic goodness. This cycle affects not only our psychological and cultural state but the economy as well. To suggest we wake up to our lives is not to suggest that we try to overcome our dampened human spirits by fostering a sense of elation, personally or culturally; rather, if humanity is to go forward, we must find a social building block that is not subject to either depression or elation.

This train of thought led me to reflect on a profound instruction from my father—that pain and joy do not arise from anywhere outside our own minds. The joy of happiness and the intensity of pain are the experiences of thoughts and emotions arising from the mind itself. We tend to approach the general experiences of happiness and suffering in a dualistic manner: Something "out there" made me happy or sad. In reality, they are generated by the mind. Therefore, how we handle our own mind is essential.

To experience a sense of release and freedom depends on our ability not to be trapped by every thought or emotion. The attitude we take toward our mind and how we moderate our thoughts and emotions is the barometer of how livable our life is. If we become angry because of what somebody has said, stewing in the thought of bitterness and revenge only tortures us. When we decide to see the falsity of our resentment, we are released from being trapped in our own pain.

The essential instruction in this process of being able to release is completely connected with the Shambhala principle: With confidence in our own worthiness, the mind has more strength, intelligence, flexibility, and magnanimity regarding its own thoughts, feelings, and opinions. This is very much what my father meant by "Cheer yourself up." When the mind feels powerless, we are more influenced by latent emotions, as well as the emotions of others. Our mind becomes easily manipulated. Out of despair, we might criticize others or ourselves. This stems from being confused about who we are. The word *cheer* is a synonym for confidence arising from our trust in basic goodness.

This deep confidence in our own worthiness helps us overcome forces of suffering such as being poisoned by our own anger, bled by desire, or stuck by our own stupidity. When these strong emotions monopolize our mindstream, we should realize that our mind has been co-opted and falsely seduced. Our anger and resentment, as well as our desire and obsession, are causing havoc on our home ground, and we are feeling the brunt of the conflict: stress, unhappiness, lack of focus, hopelessness, despair, and an overwhelming feeling of depression. This is the mind suffering due to its own thought processes concerning how to regard itself.

When the mind lacks confidence, it is more prone to duality, where our subjective and objective experiences of the world become more disparate. If we see people enjoying themselves, we feel depressed or irritated. If external challenges or opportunities arise, we quickly lose heart. When something appears to offer some salvation, we become desperate.

Conversely, losing confidence in our own worthiness can rob us of contentment. Our mind is desperately trying to leave itself behind. Wanting to separate from any feeling of self-awareness or reflectivity, it enters an elated, heightened state. Here the mind is trying to address an inner dissatisfaction by immersing itself in external stimuli. We become obsessed with excitement, thinking that gossip, entertainment, staying busy will address deep-seated issues. Although exciting events can also be good, the mind cannot heal itself by over-objectifying things and constantly latching onto external experiences.

For the mind to feel good about itself can only come about by the mind healing itself. This process of the mind healing, or redeveloping confidence in our own worthiness, can be supported and encouraged by friends, family, good advice, and insightful wisdom, but ultimately it relies on mental nourishment. Just as the body recuperates by resting and eating good food, the mind heals and gains mental strength by allowing itself to rest in its own goodness and worthiness. Just as the body naturally wants to heal itself, given the opportunity, the view of the Shambhala principle is that the mind, too, wants to heal itself, given the opportunity.

Even conventionally speaking, when something like a stranger's smile appears to cheer us up, our mind, in a split-second decision, decides to cheer up. In that moment, we release doubt, hesitation, irritation, and depression. That cheerfulness is the mind experiencing its own well-being in that moment. It can do this because some intuitive sense of our own basic goodness causes us to relax. Being naturally equipped with the networks of kindness, the pathways of forgiving, and love—as well as intelligence and generosity—we are entitled to be cheerful.

The Shambhala principle is suggesting that we build confidence in our worthiness rather than continuing to vault between depression and elation. In particular, we must let go of the preoccupied feeling that we are guilty of some fundamental mistake. Being cheerful is a way to keep our confidence steady. Appreciating where we are right now is a helpful antidote to depression. What comes from that is joy.

Part III

BEING

12

SHIFTING GLOBAL VALUES

ONE DAY WHEN I was a young boy, my father said it would be good for me to start learning how to meditate. When I asked him why, he said, "To discover the power of the mind." He also emphasized that meditation would provide a way to take responsibility for my thoughts and emotions.

In the West, we sometimes think of meditation as a way to attain alternate states of consciousness or as a means to fix something we feel is broken. In reality, meditation is about developing good mental hygiene and, at the same time, a sense of our unconditional mental health. One Tibetan word for meditation means "familiarity." In that sense, we are always meditating, for we are always becoming familiar with something.

In Buddhism, we regard the thinking mind as being fairly neutral, a space in which we can have good thoughts or bad thoughts. Even at a superficial level, those thoughts and feelings have a tremendous impact on our life. For example, one instant of feeling wronged might lead us to a lifetime driven by feeling the need for revenge. Conversely, experiencing a moment of kindness might foster a life motivated by gratitude.

Ultimately what I learned from my meditation practice was that the human mind has the ability to determine the outcome of every day. Once your mind has decided to do something, life is what follows. However, often how we feel about something is so interconnected with our social conditioning that we are unable to distinguish between our own thoughts and values and the parroting of what is socially accepted. We do not even allow ourselves to think or feel things that stray from the social norm. A lot of this is due to how we are educated, in terms of our schooling as well as our family upbringing.

As well, there is a collective human upbringing through the centuries. If we are born in the West, our values are tied in with Western history and thought. We are brought up to value individualism, and thus there is a constant need to distinguish ourselves from others. We think nothing of moving away from our own family in the pursuit of something better. In the East, we might be brought up to be more communal, and we strive to blend in with the group. However, no matter how we were raised, many ideas we consider to be our own are actually coming from social ceremonies that have been grafted onto our minds, and when we are moving through our day at a speedy pace, we may never question them.

In meditation, we are exploring how our mind really feels, unconditioned by family, education, friends, culture, and even our concepts about meditation. Resting in this space is self-empowerment minus the ego. Even so, the cultural environment has a strong influence on how we meditate. If we are constantly surrounded by a society that is telling us that we are unworthy and not good, then as we attempt to meditate and relax, inevitably we relax in our unworthiness and guilt. This is the power of culture at an intimate level. Conversely, if we are brought into a culture of basic goodness, the tendency to relax into this goodness during meditation is natural.

Therefore, even though we may be developing personal traits while meditating, the influence of society is omnipresent. The power of meditation develops a personal culture of strength. That enables us to influence not only our personal culture, but also the culture of our environment.

Individual value systems are based on what we think we are worth. Self-worth is directly linked to social worth. In order to be regarded as worthy, we may even engage in harmful actions because we are social creatures who wish to fit in to our environment. One of my spiritual colleagues,

Rabbi Irwin Kula, traveled to Rwanda in order to understand how people there could have engaged in the horrific acts of human genocide that had decimated that country. When he returned, he told me that when he asked Rwandans why they had killed, the most common answer people gave was, "Because that is what others were doing." This answer highlights in a gruesome way that we are completely responsible for our own value system but—most poignantly—that our environment and others' thoughts and actions have a big influence on our mind's inherent neutrality.

Currently, humanity as a whole may value selfishness and aggression more than care and kindness. At a global level, we are all engaged in a giant meditation on humanity's pitfalls. But collectively, we can't be naïve and think the world we live in now was created by anyone other than us. Somehow, throughout the evolution of human history, we have come to this point, and the future ceremony of humanity will be determined by what value system we next put in place.

Every day, through the power of our mind, we are setting up our own value system. There are many things happening all around us—traffic and weather, for example—that we can't control. But we can control our own intention and involvement. The meditation period is the time of the day when we train ourselves in that. We take our mind and develop it the way we want, setting our intention and becoming familiar with it.

Another Tibetan word for meditation translates as "strong mind." This means meditating on particular themes that infuse our minds with healthy habits, so we are able to sustain those qualities. If we were meditating on compassion and then we lose our temper when somebody takes a parking spot, our meditation was not very strong. We have to develop it until it is resilient and can be maintained. The most important tool for doing that is care—having respect for what we are doing. There are many techniques to cultivate mindfulness, but when we care what happens to our mind, we are naturally mindful, just as if we are protecting our own child.

Care is the lack of aggression. In the body, lack of aggression is good posture. My father taught me that good posture is the antidote to sickness. The different parts of our bodies are not struggling with one another. "With a smile on your face and good head and shoulders," he said.

In the mind, the lack of aggression means not struggling with concepts. We are no longer trying to hold everything together by drumming up some logic rather than having forward vision. Now we let it go. In meditation, "letting go" has many meanings, such as letting go of thoughts and emotions. In general, it means letting go of hanging on. What are we hanging on to? Is that who we are? Letting go of that hesitation, we feel goodness.

My father taught me that staying in touch with goodness is like riding a horse. We can learn the theories of riding a horse and be taught the need for balance, but in order to be a good rider, we need to feel the horse. We need to know how to be in the saddle, in touch with our activity. If we are not in tune, when the horse spooks, we will lose balance and be thrown off. Likewise, if we are not in tune with our mind and body, we will be caught in fantasy and, ultimately, doubt. In meditation, we reduce our activities, keep it simple, and learn to hold our seat, no matter what comes up. Our trust and conviction in basic goodness is not dislodged. Thus, good meditation occurs through instinct, just like good riding. It becomes more familiar, and its influence starts to show up in our life.

When our meditation practice shows up in our life, it is called attainment. What do we attain? We get a handle on the mind. We can look at the mind without judgment and see how it is, and we can deal with it: "I feel so envious. What can I do about that?" or more on the spot, "Goodwill or envy?" If we are aware, the envy will serve as a reminder to reconnect with a bigger mind, like contentment. Without consistently strengthening our enlightened qualities, however, it is difficult to change the course of our mind's habits when we are on the go.

With practice, we have the freedom to engage in certain thoughts or not. Now we can consider our intention in a bigger way. First, what are the principles by which we want to gauge our progress in life? We could say, "In general I want to become more understanding, cheerful, and strong; that's the direction in which I want to go." We can also have a daily check-in: "What am I highlighting today? Today I would like to be more forgiving." And we can do it. When we have strong purpose and intention, we have more energy. Our body and mind are synchronized, which gives us the power to use our life expediently and well. This synchronicity occurs because of a lack of hesitation and an openness to the world.

In this dark age, a predominant manifestation of doubt—and thus lack of bravery—is our idea that not paying attention and not having mindfulness is somehow pleasurable. Assuming that mind and body are two separate entities, we consider keeping them together to be hard work. Thus, in the addiction to finding satisfaction outside ourselves in entertainment, food, shopping, or substances, we might actually seek their *not* being synchronized. With such doubt in our inherent strength and unity, we soon realize that *un*synchronized mind and body brings infirmity, for sickness plagues the body, and disbelief plagues the mind—especially disbelief regarding basic goodness.

In truth, mind and body are inherently synchronized. We are intact now; we have always been whole. This is basic goodness. In relation to mind and body, "basic" means that the contained and the container are one. Because the belly of the vase protrudes, it is naturally synchronized with the water it contains. Because there is a nervous system, the mind naturally has a place to integrate with the body.

When a couple are united, they feel a primordial synchronicity that manifests as love. Being in sync brings a dignity that goes beyond either individual. When two beings feel this way, they glow. That completeness provides a spark for dignity to blaze. This is *ziji*, "brilliant confidence," which I mentioned earlier. It is luster brought about through synchronicity.

This element of organic chemistry applies to life as a whole. To be full human beings, we cannot simply be trapped in our minds. When the mind is empty of its fixation on "me," it is full of gentleness and humor, precision and strength, and dignity arises. Because dignity comes from being fully present, genuine dignity exudes synchronicity. Things feel right, and it shows.

At this crossroads, can we use each day to meditate and then step out the door with a focus—to be kind, to contemplate life's dreamlike quality, or to look carefully at "pleasure" before giving chase? When we do this, we are creating a sustainable internal environment that will have a potent effect on our world, for what is life but an extended day? Through the power of our global mind, we can shift our whole value system. But first we must realize the power of the mind. Next we must shift our contemplation to the goodness we already possess. Then, when we ask people why they are being kind, they will answer, "Because that is what others are doing."

13

KEEP IT SIMPLE

When I became overwhelmed, I would ask my father what to do. He said, "Keep it simple." This was one of the most powerful spiritual transmissions I ever received. He was communicating to me that I already had the answer: I could always come back to goodness.

The technique my father was offering was not complicated. I had already learned that in the midst of an argument, taking a deep breath and asking myself a question like "Exertion or laziness?" or "Jealousy or letting go?" could return me to goodness. Wisdom recognizes that the answer is already here, and simplicity is the result. In this light, the wisdom of the Shambhala principle has the power to bring true realization and meaning.

When I asked my father how to stay more in touch with basic goodness, he would encourage me to adopt an attitude of wakefulness. He said, "You should wake yourself up in the morning, even if you feel tired." It was his way of communicating the power of thought. To wake ourselves up is to feel what is always in our hearts, and to stay awake is to embody it throughout the day. If we lose the connection, our activity will be at the mercy of whatever emotions are around, and life will become complicated. Every moment has its energy; either it will ride us, or we can ride it.

My father would often tell me, "Hold your seat." Again, his instruction was to maintain confidence in my inner strengths. The Shambhala approach is that discursive thoughts and strong emotions become harmful and confusing only because they exacerbate our feelings of insecurity and inadequacy. According to Mencius, holding our seat is not straying from our good heart. Socrates also speaks of this theme: "For a good man, no evil is possible. Whether he be dead or alive, no evil is possible." Learning to relax with the goodness in our hearts, we will become more skilled at recognizing it everywhere else.

It is important not to overthink the problem. Through overanalyzing the world's issues, we become depressed and lose faith because we are no longer in touch with windhorse, the ability to attain success that comes from acting virtuously. My father told me, "As a warrior, you should clean up your act. Simply work on the spot, properly. Very straightforward." With this approach, simple can understand complicated because it knows that it contains the answer, but complicated cannot understand simple because it doesn't know it exists.

Simplicity indicates that a particular feeling resonates with us in a very deep way: We are hungry and we want to eat, we are tired and we want to rest, we are dirty and we want to shower, we are lonely and we want a relationship. At the root of these most basic elements of life is a greater simplicity: We all want success and happiness, and we'd like to be free of fear and pain. However, obtaining these simple objectives can get complicated.

When my father said, "Keep it simple," he was not instructing me to ignore the world's complications, but to be strong and demonstrate the principles I had studied and contemplated. Simplicity became the notion of conviction—a feeling of being completely singular in my mental prowess. It is like shooting an arrow: One focuses, one aims, and all peripheral hesitation drops away. In the Shambhala teachings, the arrow represents the intelligence of a completely confident warrior. Most of life's challenges can be met with a mind that is simple and confident in its principle. For example, approaching a relationship with a mind of wholehearted kindness or generosity often allows it to progress. Therefore, simplicity is an indication of the strength and health of the mind.

The ability to solve complicated matters comes down to simply understanding each point thoroughly. As each point is understood, the overall structure of the complication begins to weaken. Therefore, by telling me to keep it simple, my father was teaching me how to prioritize. Along those lines, he said that the curious thing about wisdom is that it is interconnected. We do not have to study all knowables. However, by understanding one piece of wisdom we immediately gain access to all wisdom. This also applies to the notion of virtue. By understanding kindness, we gain insight into generosity, which in turn helps us understand prudence and temperance, through which we gain access to mindfulness and therefore intelligence.

Conversely, once we begin to lie, then cheating is not far off, and theft and other harmful habits are waiting in the wings. The Shambhala principle sees these negative traits not as a reflection of our inherent character, but rather as a sign that we lack confidence in our wisdom and worthiness.

When we are overwhelmed by complication, we sometimes throw in the towel and give up on the whole endeavor. In hindsight, we realize that if we had been a bit more patient or generous, or applied a bit more exertion, success was at hand. Keeping it simple is determining and relying upon whatever positive mental and emotional qualities we have in any given moment—however faint they may be. For example, if we are at work and overwhelmed by deadlines, we can in that moment keep it simple by applying exertion, cheerfulness, and maybe even generosity.

When my father said, "Keep it simple," he was giving me instruction on simplicity as a method for enhancing my confidence. Humanity could now use this simple instruction. When we do not feel confident in our simple worthiness to be here on the planet Earth, the world becomes infinitely complicated as we attempt to placate some unresolved inner dilemma about our own existence.

In this light, the world has evolved in its complexity, especially now that we are more aware of how other people live. By seeing different ways of living, questions naturally begin to arise about life's purpose and meaning. As a child in Tibet, my father wondered what kind of robes people in neighboring regions might wear, or how they might herd their yaks. He was once given a clock made in England, and wondered what kind of people created it. Now, with the television and Internet, within a few minutes we can watch parts of a horse race in Mongolia, a soccer match in England, a documentary on tribal life in the Amazon, a news story unfolding in the Middle East, and a reality show in California. Seeing all these images, we may be entertained, but underneath we are trying to understand the notion of existence altogether: What is it to be human? What is a sane way to live on this earth?

In asking these questions, we are like the pre-Socratic

thinkers and the Buddha trying to come to terms with the nature of existence. However, the society in which we live now is more porous. It is much easier for the rich and the poor to see how each other live; likewise for the developed and undeveloped countries. Even though there are still great differences between cultures and traditions, more than ever we are exposed to the total experience of humanity trying to exist on this earth. As cultural differences become challenged by cultural similarities, having confidence in humanity becomes the way to keep it simple. Acknowledging our worthiness and goodness, we can share it with others as a universally human expression.

Thus, in this time of great complication, it is through the fearless and simple message of basic goodness that we can understand the heart of the matter. With such simplicity, all answers are revealed and all questions fall away.

14

COMING FULL CIRCLE

IN 2001—AND AGAIN in 2004—I journeyed to Tibet, more than forty years after my father had left. I wanted to reconnect with the deep spiritual and cultural roots of my ancestral homeland. My visits were a curious journey of cross-pollination. I returned to Tibet carrying photos of my father and teachings that he had composed since he had fled Tibet in 1959. At the same time, I was welcomed as an influential teacher in my own right, as the reincarnation of the renowned nineteenth-century teacher Mipham the Great, and as the sakyong of Shambhala. I met members of my family. I visited King Gesar's tromping ground and the location of his palace. Some cosmic symbiotic adventure was surely taking place.

On that first trip to Tibet, I was able to walk in the hills where my father had walked, and meditate in some of the same caves and meadows. I was profoundly affected by sitting in these desolate and lonely sacred places, where meditators had contemplated the nature of humanity for the last eight hundred years. Although the meditation tradition is ancient, it has endured because humanity has not changed. Our questions about who we are and how we feel about ourselves are as relevant today as they were centuries ago.

As I sat in those caves, I realized one thing: In that bleak, rugged climate, no one did anything frivolously. Meditation was not a spiritual dalliance; it was vital to life, like food or water. Sitting there, I became aware of its original intent—to provide a period for strengthening one's feeling and trust of basic goodness. It is a practical way of tuning into the essence of life and the central force of our being. That is how unconditional goodness became the blueprint for daily life at the height of Tibetan culture.

In speaking of basic goodness, it is important to share how Tibetan tantric Buddhism arrived at such a conclusion. Even though I believe that basic goodness is universal—and that many religions, as well as philosophical systems, have reached the same conclusion—in our particular tradition, exposition on the topic has been prolific, filling thousands of volumes of profound texts.

COMING FULL CIRCLE } 131

The apex of profound teaching, the Great Perfection, reveals the inherent nature of the mind. In this system of thought, the mind is divided into two areas: relative mind and ultimate mind. The ultimate mind is regarded as wisdom, and the relative mind is regarded as intelligence, the expression of that wisdom.

The relative mind is the basis of the ultimate. The ultimate mind is the basis of the relative. In the Great Perfection, at the highest levels of transmission, the relative and ultimate are revealed to be inseparable in their nature, basic goodness.

The relative—or "referential"—mind functions through a process of duality; therefore the relative mind always has subject and object. Thus, the dualistic mind is the conceptual mind, with the subject of "me" and the object of "other." Gathering various attributes of consciousness and body, the mind has arrived at a strange conclusion: a bundle known as a "self." Rather than feel the free-flowing quality of perceptions and experiences, the mind has consolidated them into one entity—all because it could not handle interdependence. From that moment it has based all experiences upon this identity called "me." Similarly, this self regards others not as interdependent, but as separate selves.

Because forcing these disparate elements into "me" is unnatural, trying to hold the concept together always causes tension, and the natural outcome is further tension. When others threaten this tension called "me," the concept becomes angry. When others cater to and flatter this concept, it wants to draw in the praise, and desire is added to the mix. When others' self-fabrications have more finesse, this self cannot handle it, becoming envious. Thus, the self became a perpetual universe of push and pull. In fact, to continue its storyline it needs to fabricate a universe in which to act out its fantasy, which results in the process of birth, aging, and death. However, no matter what universe it fabricates, the concept of self is always in pain.

In meditation, we use this dualistic mind to focus on an object such as a feeling or the breath. In such a practice we are beginning to reflect on the mind's true nature. We observe that we are constantly vacillating between relative—our conceptual way of seeing—and ultimate—the nature of things as they are, free of concept. On a relative level, it appears that we exist here and now. There's a "me" who has feelings and emotions. There's a world of sentient beings and material goods ("the other"). But that world is in a constant state of flux and disintegration. Anger, jealousy, and fixation are all created by our mind's belief that appearances are real. Ultimately the material world does not exist in the way we think. It appears to exist because we hold it together with our minds. So in this kind of practice we look at the mind and its tendency to cling to appearances.

It is said that the dualistic mind has eight levels of consciousness. Generally, we are not aware of these, even though we are constantly experiencing them. We connect with the world with the consciousness of each of the five senses: taste, touch, smell, sight, and sound. The sixth sense consciousness is how we think about the world: Do we like something? Do we not like it? Do we care? The seventh consciousness is known as the afflicted consciousness: Its affliction is pride. The Tibetan word for pride means "I am glorious," and it enhances the tendency to see oneself as a separate, solid entity. This consciousness sits there all day long saying, "This is 'me' and I am real," imposing that dualistic concept of self on everything that happens.

The eighth consciousness, the most elusive, is the vast, deep consciousness where all experiences are held, known as "the ground basis for all." It is said that the eighth consciousness is like fertile soil, and that the others are like seeds constantly being planted in that soil. When those seeds are planted, they sprout and grow. This is known as cause and effect—in Sanskrit, *karma,* or action. Karma occurs as we see, hear, smell, taste, and touch—and especially as we produce thoughts and emotions in response to those perceptions.

These thoughts make up what most of what we regard as our mind. It experiences something "out there," objectifies it, and from that, a thought or opinion arises. For example, we smell lamb stew, and we like it, but then we see that it has carrots and potatoes in it, and we don't like it. Since this dualistic experience is constantly happening, concepts, habits, feelings, and emotions are constantly arising. They are all embedded in the eighth consciousness, which is similar to what Western psychology calls the unconscious.

Beyond these forms of dualistic mind lies the ultimate— or "nonreferential"—mind. In my philosophical tradition this is known as wisdom. The Tibetan word for it means "knowing from the beginning." It indicates that from the beginning of time, the human mind has contained profound knowledge. We humans are not ignorant.

How does this wisdom know? According to the teaching of the Great Perfection, wisdom has two inherent qualities that allow it to be omniscient. The first is great space, or emptiness. This emptiness is not negation or blankness; it means "empty of ignorance," or "empty of not knowing." It refers to the feeling of being without boundaries, and without a reference point. It is free of anxiety, worry, and doubt, and therefore it is full of luminosity. This is essentially a synonym for knowing; it is described as brilliant. Wisdom is therefore regarded as the inseparability of space and brilliance.

This unique combination has been described in many ways. Upon attaining enlightenment, when asked what he had experienced, the Buddha said that it was beyond words, but then he proceeded to describe it as the union of emptiness and luminosity. In Buddhism, this perpetually arising wisdom is called "ground tantra." According to tantra, we do not become enlightened—we discover our enlightenment, which has always been here. In the Shambhala texts, this is called "the dawning of humanity," or the Great Eastern Sun.

The Great Eastern Sun is the forward-moving windhorse principle, that perpetual morning inspiration. It is living life with vision and inspiration. That is the energy we can bring into our lives, where it illuminates everything and disperses any shadows of the setting sun. We do this by the process of contemplation, or "bringing to mind." Then, as my father said, "It just zooms into you, enters into your heart."

What keeps us from tasting our inherent wisdom? Concept. Concept is what we add to the interdependent nature of things. Moment by moment we look at ourselves and the world, solidifying our impermanent perceptions and feelings into a particular view of our own that colors everything we do and plants seeds for the future. When we die, this concept of self—which we had assumed to be this body with this family and these friends—dissolves, and only consciousness remains. That is very destabilizing.

This matrix of concept that we take as a self comes in many variations, but its weak point is always the same: It is fabricated. In general, we are chasing one conceptual creation after another. Without really looking at the nature of appearances, we project a meaning-generality onto the world, shaping it with our assumption of independent existence. In our current environment of social degeneration and ethical instability, in the storm of such concept, basic goodness has become the echo of a whisper we can barely hear.

However, within our discursiveness, we are perpetually looking for something that will make us happy. Instinctively we know that there is satisfaction to be found; we just don't know where to look for it. This is a sign that our intelligence and enlightenment are always at play. Yet, if we are unaware that we contain wisdom and, therefore, consider life to be simply a matter of physical gratification, then naturally our minds will put their energy into producing endless material objects to satisfy our sense perceptions.

The question often arises, "How can a deep period of stillness and contemplation have any relevance to daily life and current world issues?" Or, in the same light, "What does ancient philosophy have to do with modern life?"

Meditation practice is relevant because in meditation our conceptual mind relaxes and we can feel who we are at heart. Can we settle into our own being and appreciate it? If we sit down with the inspiration "I have to *do* something" and hope the meditation will help, to a certain degree it can help, but there is an innate incongruity in this approach: We are meditating when we're unsatisfied with who we are. Because we cannot feel our goodness, we can't simply be, and we end up in a distracted state. In order to reverse it, Shambhala combines meditative insight with social application, and it begins with being properly on the spot. That is one of the biggest issues we currently face. Therefore, when we sit down and feel our worthiness, it is not just *us* sitting down—it is the entire world sitting down.

This is the cultural dichotomy I inhabit: ancient and modern, meditative and engaged. I feel that the understanding of consciousness according to the metaphysics of my tradition—or the philosophical traditions of ancient Greece or ancient China or India—is as relevant today as it was then. In addition, we now have the understanding of modern science.

Science and spirituality are both here to provide a cultural setting in which humanity can try to understand itself. From the diversity of classical gods to what biologists see under the microscope, all common realities have shared a search for the meaning of life. One pivotal point of the discussion is the relationship between relative and absolute, logical and mystical, duality and nonduality. Science and spirituality may seem to separate at this juncture. Simultaneously, this seems to be the juncture where empirical analysis and faith intersect, as science is beginning to recognize the beneficial effects of meditation.

Humanity now finds itself at this very intersection, and confusion has arisen. An underlying assumption from the time of Francis Bacon to the present is that if something cannot be seen, or unequivocally proven, then fundamentally it does not exist. Our science is based on empirical proof. However, that proof is ultimately based on our perception. The Shambhala teachings are saying that by using our perceptions, we can tap into the un-nameable energy of life itself.

Can science and technology somehow resolve the dilemma between relative and absolute? Is there anything to trust beyond what we can prove? Can we join the scientific culture with a meditative culture?

The Great Perfection tells us that relative and absolute are one and the same, and my father once said that their union was his specialty. That is a key element of the Shambhala principle, which is saying that the highest truth is here now, in the most ordinary way. The Shambhala path is neither conventionally spiritual nor conventionally secular. The path is rich because it is not just about how much we meditate. It relates with how we dress, how we eat, how we converse, how we buy, and how we sell. We bring the view of sacredness and spirit into relating with our day. My father explained it this way: "You might have mindfulness and awareness happening all the time. But on top of that, you have to keep up with your actual day-to-day life."

However, if we overemphasize the relative, we lose vision, and life becomes materialistic. Humanity is seen simply as cruel, and fear rules our actions. If we overemphasize the ultimate, we lose practicality and fill our world with intangible gods and the afterlife. By working with the mind, we align our spiritual aspirations with our daily lives for the benefit of the future. With the Shambhala principle, we can do it.

When I returned to Tibet, I tried to bring this message to the people who came to hear my teachings—that human nature as discovered and experienced by my father and other meditators in those hills is not something to be relegated to the past. Basic goodness is as here now as it was then. This conclusion about our worthiness that arose from their ancestors' practice of meditation is a most precious heritage for the world. The journey of basic goodness has come full circle.

15

NOW

ONE DAY, I asked my father if I would become enlightened, and he said, "Yes." I asked, "When?" And he said, "Now." For a young boy, it was a puzzling answer. I thought he was playing with me, yet I felt a strong message coming through. As I continued my education in meditation, I was caught by the spell of hope there, too—never really applying my practice to this moment, but always thinking that my enlightenment would happen in the future. When my understanding and experience grew, I began to realize what my father meant by *now*. It began to dawn on me that enlightenment can happen only in the now, for enlightenment is the moment when we completely recognize who we are. That is always possible, but only now.

I would often receive this transmission of nowness from my father. Sometimes he called it *being*. He would say, "Let's be." Then gently he would hold my hand and look at me, and a great relaxation would occur—a feeling of warmth, depth, and simplicity. Sometimes he would then say, "Good." In that moment, he was transmitting basic goodness. On the one hand, a powerful spiritual transmission was being given. On the other, we were simply father and son sitting there, relaxing together.

When my father held my hand, he was giving me an ordinary human transmission: If we can feel, then we can simply *be*. Basic goodness is not abstract; it is alive and runs throughout our whole being. The world is fresh and full of warmth and love, and humanity is gifted at experiencing it. From this open and sensitive state, we communicate. It is the wellspring from which we create great music and art, great commerce, economics, and politics. The Zen tradition addresses this notion of nowness, as did the ancient Greeks and Marcus Aurelius, the philosopher emperor of Rome. Each of these cultures understood that nowness has tremendous power—as in the Shambhala tradition of windhorse.

The ancient stoic philosophers worked with this principle. The Taoist sages called it the Way. Whatever we call it, there is, within the continuum of time and space, a clear and perfect ever-present moment that is whole and singular. *Now* is humanity coming into contact with its beating heart. In the Great Perfection this is known as heart essence. In Shambhala it is called the *Ashe*. The present, the singular, the now, is not a fleeting moment. Rather, in that moment, the absolute and relative, the micro and the macro, are completely held.

The theory of the Big Bang is that the entire universe was produced from one small but dense particle of energy. As the heat of the explosion cooled, the universe was created. Thus, every time we experience the elements—the way the earth smells after it rains, the dry heat of summer air—we are experiencing the beginning of time. We naturally come into contact with our origin and, thus, our goodness. In the same way, when we see stars and galaxies or embrace each other, we are touching the beginning of the Big Bang.

The Tibetan word for basic goodness refers to this sense of timelessness, for it literally means "primordial goodness." Our nature transcends time altogether. It is not confined by space, for there is no relativity to it—it is neither small nor big. *Primordial* means "beginningless." However, the beginning is not some long ago time when our goodness was born; it refers to this very moment: Our goodness is being born now.

Throughout time, sages have described this notion of birth—and therefore origin—sometimes as beginningless and sometimes as having a beginning. However, in Shambhala, the beginning—the prime, or first, or principle—refers to the fact that our birth is perpetually occurring from goodness. It is not that we were previously bad, and now we are becoming good. "Prime" means that from the beginningless beginning, we are good. This factor is critical, because if there were a beginning, there would have to be an end, and then our nature would not be primordial. Therefore, basic goodness is beyond any timeline, and can be known only now. Our awakening is currently exploding. The Big Bang of our consciousness is happening at this very instant. Beyond beginning and end, our enlightenment is perpetually happening.

The transmission of nowness happens when we have confidence in our own awakening, our own perfection, our own singularity of doubtlessness. In order to experience our unconditional goodness, we must have total relaxation—a combination of confidence and vulnerability. We do not have to be anything apart from who we are. We can just be. In the Shambhala tradition, this perpetual feeling of innocence is called freshness. I see this quality in my mother, Lady Könchok Paldrön, who moved to the West in 1993. She is very childlike in her curiosity, and we tease each other. It feels like an important transmission of the culture of nowness. With this unadulterated naïveté, we are sharing our open nature, like sunlight coming through the clouds.

The opportunity to feel this tenderness is humanity's most precious gift. It makes us flexible. We can find it just by raising our eyes and looking out the window, if we relax. It is a matter of being fully engaged and taking the time to feel. When our senses become scattered, we feel speedy and disconnected and numb. We become harder, less adaptive, and less available. When we ride the moment, our mind and body are effortlessly synchronized, and that synchronicity extends to the environment.

Since our modern culture values entertainment so highly, being in the now is often very challenging for us. In fact, being in the present has been successfully branded as boring by those who doubt our nature and are constantly looking for an exit. Yet what always struck me about my father was that even when nothing was going on, it seemed like everything was going on because his presence was so genuine. This is the power of nowness. On the other hand, everything can be going on and it can feel like nothing is going on, because we're not really there.

When I asked my father how I could help the world, he said, "With nowness." Nowness is where we find life. Without this understanding, we tend to be overwhelmed by life's both positive and negative aspects. Even though our nature is beyond good and bad, if our attitude is that things are fundamentally bad, we can never handle the good, and if we try for only a good life, we can never handle the bad. But when we experience life from the ground of basic goodness—now—we are able to accommodate all the occurrences that arise.

I am a great believer in cause and effect, or karma. By opening our hearts now, we are planting a seed for a future society where "worthy" is the norm. We begin by not having any preconceptions. As brave as we have to be to try this, I ask my students to enter every situation with an open mind, which means not rejecting our feelings. We just feel how we feel now. If we feel good, it is good good. If we feel bad, it is bad good. How can this be? Because we are accepting the totality as it arises from our nature, which is worthy.

As more of us discover our goodness, it will reverberate, and good society will occur, creating perpetual inspiration, movement, and success. Nowness will be celebrated. It will become the basis of schools and education, the economy, and even agriculture. This will happen because humanity has consciously reactivated its goodness, the latent power within all our everyday drama, speed, and stress. Nowness is the union of the spiritual and the mundane. It is the union of masculine and feminine, old and young. Nowness dissolves past and future, up and down, right and wrong.

This is the ancient transmission of nowness that I experienced with my father as we held hands, gazed at each other, and felt the cool breeze and the warm sun. At that moment, he and I were an enlightened society—two humans touching their goodness, feeling vulnerable yet powerful, and unafraid to share it. In that moment of simply being, enlightenment was happening now.

16

CULTURE

THE FIRST TIME my father taught me the art of calligraphy, I was moved by the power of simply holding a brush in my hand and dipping it into ink, creating a symbol on a white sheet of paper. As I held the brush, my father held my hand. I felt his breath on my neck. As he guided my hand down the sheet of paper, I could feel a surge of power and nervous energy. When I completed my stroke, he looked at me and said, "Good." It was a curious moment of confirmation, for he was not simply saying that what I had done was good; he was also saying that my action had allowed goodness to arise.

When I asked my father why I needed to learn an ancient art like calligraphy, he said, "Enlightened culture."

In this simple act of teaching me calligraphy, he was passing along an ancient lineage of artistic expression, initiating me into his culture of goodness. He wanted to bring sophistication to a young boy, and through this artistic ritual, he was contributing to my cultural self-identity. He felt that painting, poetry, music, and dance are ways we can come into contact with that goodness. Even Aristotle talks about art being the truest expression of nature. Therefore, art is considered to be one of the highest hallmarks of civilized culture. It communicates basic goodness through symbol, which gives others the power to realize it instantaneously, without language.

Culture helps us recognize and nurture the good in ourselves, others, and in society at large. Family recipes, prepared with love and care; a father teaching his son a song his own father sang to him; a mother teaching her daughter the family trade—these are the sculptors of social identity, the mechanism by which we understand our place in the world.

The Latin word for culture, *colere*, means "to cultivate." In the classical period, culture was linked to the notion of cultivation in agriculture, where a seed is cultivated in order to grow. Culture was considered to be the moisture and sunlight needed for humanity's seeds of intelligence, kindness, temperance, and patience to grow. In the modern vernacular, *culture* can mean the humanities or art—what might be considered the "softer" elements of modern education as opposed to science or engineering, which might be considered "hard," or more essential, building blocks of modernity. The classical use of the word was more all-encompassing. Developing as a human meant that one would study art as well as science. One would learn a trade as well as philosophy. Our modern culture is more influenced by technology and science, and less by agriculture and art. With the emphasis on what is important, culture is being transmitted.

Culture is the invisible network humanity creates that allows us to understand and develop meaning. Values, ethics, and ideas are being transmitted through communal osmosis, a very potent expression that is not as linear and dogmatic as other forms of education. Just like the intent of the mind, the expression is omnipresent but cannot be found. In this light, culture has a strong influence on all of us, both individually and collectively.

Creating an enlightened culture based on the direct display of basic goodness has the power to shift the world's future. In turn, such a culture can become the environmental support for fostering valiant principles. Thus, developing personal and social environments that manifest, engender, and support the values at our core is critical to creating enlightened society. If we simply try to isolate ourselves through meditation and other methods of self-development, without addressing the culture of our societies, we may make personal progress toward peace.

But if we are living in an aggressive and speedy society, it will be challenging to change it by activating the deeper principles we have cultivated.

A culture can be created around a single entity or product. For example, in Tibet, China, and Japan, as well as in England and Russia, tea became the expression, as well as the progenitor, of culture. Beyond just a method to stay awake, serving tea—how the water was boiled, how the tea was poured, what utensils were used, which food was served—became a way to transmit value, ethics, and intelligence, as well as sophistication. Like humanity itself, tea was considered precious. In Tibet, it was used as currency. In Japan, houses were built in which to drink the tea, allowing for rest and renewal. Now coffee has created a culture as well, with coffee shops an essential feature of modern life. Whether one drinks coffee or tea, their cultures communicate a feeling of warmth, an expression of being awake and alive, and the notion of hearth—a place to gather, celebrate, and communicate.

Since the mind can endlessly produce thoughts, clearly it has the potential to endlessly produce new products. Like thoughts, they may not necessarily be helpful or beneficial. In the past, technological culture-changers like the telephone and electricity took a long time to produce; as well, cultures had more time to absorb and contemplate their impact. Now, especially with electronic media, new cultural and ethical values are being developed and challenged, and things are changing so fast that we have little time to contemplate and absorb their impact.

Like many other things, technology can serve us well or not serve us well. If we approach it with vision, we can utilize it. If we lack vision, technology can prey on us, detecting our weakness or lack of resolve, such as discursiveness or desire for gossip. Or it distracts us from nowness. In this way, it seduces us for a few minutes, which become hours, days, months, and years.

We can tell if we have been served well by technology if we feel uplifted, informed, or delighted by it. These are signs that the encounter was virtuous. However, if we feel dull or disconnected, then clearly that technology has numbed our senses. We are mentally less sharp, and emotionally distant. We know we were used by the technology, as opposed to using it, because it has drained our energy and weakened our windhorse. Technology can be a great expeditor of virtue, or it can create negativity. With the telephone or email, we can easily comfort, console, or celebrate with others. At the same time, because we are not face-to-face, we might say or do things that we would not normally say or do. Thus, our negativity can become exponential due to the effect and power of technology. We may also tend to hide behind the electronic medium because we are less exposed.

Even though technology has advanced our ability to

communicate, the five basic parameters of karma are still in place: raising the intention, deciding to do the action, preparing to do the action, doing the action, and having no regret. We can decide to either apologize or to chastise an individual, and once the "send" button is pushed, the karma has been initiated. Afterward, if we sit there satisfied, it is a complete karmic act. That action does not go unnoticed.

In the modern era we need to be even more convinced of virtue, having resolve in terms of who we are and how we want to manifest. Generally, the best approach with technology is to consider our dignity and concern for others. By engaging in negative actions using technology, we forsake our dignity, and the harm to others becomes exponential.

Thus, as we produce new programs for our laptops and applications for our smartphones, the principles of virtue must be clear in our minds. We must have the resolve and inspiration to manifest it; otherwise, we are easily reduced into the lower modes of behavior. The point is to cherish the mind and not abuse it. If we remain mindful of our principles and priorities, just as we do in meditation, we can use technology to awaken our discipline and dignity, instead of letting it take over our lives.

My father told me that his favorite word was *discipline*. When I was doing solitary retreat in the mountains, one of the most important instructions he gave me was that if I was going to be alone, I was responsible for creating my own strong culture within the confines of my meditation cabin. That meant maintaining a good daily schedule and paying attention to bathing and dressing, eating and cleaning even though no one could see what I was doing. Discipline and dignity bind us to our senses and surroundings. Without them we move toward insanity instead of enlightenment.

Culture is contagious. Our association with it is like a giant self. Without having to think, we know how others feel, and we react to experiences in similar ways. Therefore encountering someone from another culture can be frightening or awkward; it is challenging to communicate. We don't trust what we don't know. Naturally, as human beings become threatened, they dig in deeper.

My father talked about the need for cultural curiosity and appreciating interdependence—in part, no doubt, reflecting upon what had happened in his own country. Ironically, for a Buddhist culture steeped in the principle of interdependence, Tibet's policy toward the rest of the world was isolationist. The nation was unaware of global events, thereby becoming a victim of its own failure to see its interconnectedness with the rest of the world.

If our version of globalization is to simply promote our own culture, we are talking about imperialism, hegemony, or domination—not globalization. In this light, no culture is global, in that to be global is to accommodate diversity.

So what are we to do when there are such physical, linguistic, and spiritual differences; theists, nontheists, agnostics, materialists, anarchists, and capitalists all vying for position, power, and resources? How are we to communicate across cultural boundaries?

The best way to be global is to proclaim goodness by openheartedly extending faith in human dignity. Such faith transmits the message that through view, self-reflection, and behavior, the mind can be directed toward any goal. With these three elements, we can create a state of war, or we can create a state of peace. In creating a state of war, we view others as the enemy, and we practice how to destroy them. In creating a state of peace, we view others as ourselves, and we develop a good society by being "friendly to ourselves and merciful to others," as my father put it. Whether or not we can understand one another linguistically, culturally, and emotionally, if we all have an immovable conviction in our worthiness to occupy the human heart, then naturally we will feel connected. We can use our interconnectedness to cultivate human dignity—the bedrock of all diversity.

However, if we fail to see global interdependence and diversity as positive binding factors, it will be hard to build a culture of kindness. If we keep pointing fingers at one another, the human family will be weakened. Instead we could self-reflect, apply the view of goodness, and extend something positive. When things get rough, the warrior rises higher by being on the spot. For example, in an argument with a colleague, we can tell ourselves, "Patience, not anger." Rising above the negative emotion uplifts ourselves and the other person, and brightens the environment. My father called this illuminating ability "a sense of splendidness." Our confidence in basic goodness has matured. Like most things that are meaningful, this takes time.

In strengthening the global family, we will need to learn to communicate by learning to feel the heart. We are living in a culture where the concepts of kindness and love can seem futile, especially against greed and aggression. In our modern world, it may be hard to trust qualities that cannot be hurried, measured, or even located. Yet these intangible forces have the power to bind us. By using them, our trust in them will grow, and we will all be stronger.

Activating the Shambhala principle, we can transform the feeling of worthlessness into worthiness, ignorance into intelligence, and doubt into confidence. As a result, we can transform aggression into compassion, which eradicates fear. Out of fearlessness, we can create a world where we are all in our own diverse ways perpetually cultivating the wisdom and strength of the human family.

As I completed my first calligraphy stroke, I felt that I had witnessed the birth of understanding human nature. My father told me it was a good beginning, but that

I would have to repeat the stroke many times in order to become a master. I realized that this is what we need to do—continue to draw the stroke of worthiness and confidence until we all become masters at expressing our humanity.

Part IV

TOUCHING

17

THE ECONOMY

ONE DAY, I asked my father how I could deepen my understanding of enlightened society. He replied, "Study economics." Surprised, I asked, "Why?" He said, "It is important to understand who made the bread we eat and the clothes we wear." I was in the stage of my training to be a sakyong where I was learning a great deal about the metaphysics of the mind. With this answer, he seemed to be instructing me to take my studies further and apply my abstract understanding to the practicalities of life.

In any society, the economic system is composed of relationships in which we express our principles through conduct. The dynamics between people are determined by our attitude regarding ourselves—and in turn, regarding others. The basis of that interplay and behavior is the mind.

As I followed my father's instructions, it became apparent to me that our present economy is strongly influenced by the minds of a few great thinkers on human nature. Their conclusions—whether humans were worthy of trust or mistrust—laid the foundation for the economy's design. I discovered that economics are always connected to views of human nature: Are we generous or self-interested? Adam Smith's two greatest works straddle the dividing line between morality and economy, with his *Theory of Moral Sentiments* emphasizing the fact that humans are capable of tremendous sympathy and kindness, and *The Wealth of Nations* emphasizing self-interest as the basis of a free-market economy. Despite Smith's deeply ethical views, the modern economy now presumes that we are all fundamentally selfish and competitive. As a culture, we seem to draw the conclusion that even though it is good to be virtuous, human nature is greedy. This becomes a self-fulfilling prophecy. When we see how the economy fosters and rewards individual and corporate greed, we conclude that acting with virtue goes against our own nature and the nature of our economic system. This is not a neutral approach. If it is true, then acting with kindness and generosity cannot be sustained, as those virtues are at odds with our DNA.

This powerful example shows how assumptions about

human nature have real-world impacts. An economy based on selfishness can only become more selfish and aggressive, and when everyone is feeling assaulted by the force of greed, the qualities of trust, empathy, and generosity begin to feel unnatural.

I asked myself, How could humanity endure if goodness were merely a theory grafted onto an inherently bad foundation? The bottom line of this particular dark age is that we believe there is something wrong with us, or that we are not good enough, or that we are flawed in our very being. If we feel an undeniable, unequivocal belief in humanity's badness, then any philosophical, spiritual, or scientific approach to civilizing humanity will seem naïve and misguided. As people might say in the vernacular, "Let's get real." This feeling indicates that we associate reality with defectiveness and misery.

All the world's great thinkers have acknowledged suffering. The Buddha expressed that the natural course of human life is fraught with misery: We will all experience birth, aging, sickness, and death. However, the reality of suffering does not mean that it is the purpose and meaning of life. Within that same mind and heart that experience suffering, there is a treasure to be discovered—wisdom and kindness just waiting to be awakened and expressed.

In this light, the theistic traditions tell us that people are the children of God, or made in the image of God. Like children, we may misbehave and do bad things, but we are descendants of some deep and divine principle. The ancient Greeks called this *arête,* or "virtue." It is closely connected to the word that means "noble." For the Greeks, virtue did not necessarily mean being convinced to adopt good habits or better behavior. Rather, they used the word to describe some core attributes that reflect our nobility as human beings. The four root virtues—prudence, temperance, justice, and courage—were not imposed on the Greeks as decorum to keep them civilized; rather, they were celebrated as the best ways for people to be. The Buddhist teachings refer to this potential as a jewel, priceless and beyond measure—but often hidden. Virtues arise when we act on our nobility, our humanity, or *vir.* In the Shambhala tradition, far from regarding virtue as a matter of managing or suppressing our energy, we regard it as windhorse, the energy of success.

These themes of virtue are also prevalent in the Chinese tradition of Confucianism. After recognizing humanity's goodness, the Chinese sage Mencius, who lived at the time of the warring states, spent his life traveling and tutoring rulers of various kingdoms, trying to convince them that if they were confident in goodness, the result would be peace. When people discover their goodness, they act with virtue. Thus, virtue is the agent of our goodness.

However, even in ancient China there were systems of thought stating that humanity wants only to fulfill its desire and lust. According to Mencius, when we humans do not feel what is in our hearts, we stray from the original heart of goodness, which always leads to conflict. Mencius felt that if we continuously maintain a connection with our heart, we can enjoy life without being fooled by aggression and desire. If we have confidence in our basic goodness and maintain contact with it, experiencing the world's food and drink and life's other pleasures does not jeopardize our integrity. Therefore, engaging in virtue is not simply removing oneself from worldly pleasures.

What do all these views have to do with the economy? The economy can be seen either as the most powerful and visceral display of human selfishness, or as the manifest dynamic potential of human connectivity and community. We live in a time when we think that humanity is a depleted resource. Naturally, this influences our economy. At this critical time, if we enact the relationship between personal human worth and the flow of currency, then the basis of economic progress founded on innate human values can arise. This is an essential building block for creating enlightened society.

When my father encouraged me to contemplate the relationship between economics and basic goodness, I realized that he was trying to get me to see how basic goodness flows dynamically through society—and how the economy is a tangible and direct experience of this. All aspects of life can be approached with the view of basic goodness.

Our daily livelihood can be completely integrated with a personal and social vision. This demonstrates that money and wealth do not always imply a motivation of selfishness or greed. By changing the financial paradigm and reexamining the inherent meaning and purpose of money, we discover a powerful contemplation and method for establishing a more holistic economy. When we each infuse society with our personal worthiness and richness, we see it flow in the form of "virtue economics": The economy is the flow of virtue within society. By participating in such an economy, we are testifying to the outrageous power of the Shambhala principle.

The English word *economy* comes from the Greek word *oikonomia*, which means "the management of the household." By infusing our household and daily life with our conviction in basic goodness, we are "taking our seat," as my father would say. Applying values like generosity and discipline to our livelihood, finances, and family time becomes a pivotal step in how we understand basic goodness and bring it into our life—and therefore into our society. As my father would put it, "You can't abandon your life." He was telling me that every detail presents an opportunity to engage fully in expressing one's principles.

In our households, if we foster values based on goodness—like patience and humor—they will flow into our relationships with others in our communities, eventually influencing our nations, and finally, the rest of the world. In turn, society at every level will become a support for our own confidence in basic goodness. The economy will become a powerful display of virtue, and at the same time, it will foster virtue in individual experience. That is how humanity's inner treasure will become a richness that is shared by all.

18

PRINCIPLES OF POWER
AND WEALTH

ONE OF THE many things I admired about my father was that every moment with him was a learning experience. We could be doing the most mundane activity, and he would have a lesson for me to learn. In our periodic shopping trips, which he called "shopping expeditions," my father's intention was to teach me how to explore the world and appreciate life's finer things. I learned that an object's value is not necessarily related to its price. Certain objects have what he described as *yün*—a Tibetan word meaning "enriching presence." In the Shambhala tradition, *yün* is a goodness and power that we feel in our environment.

Even though he had grown up wearing traditional Tibetan robes, once he moved to the West, my father began to wear Western clothes. He particularly enjoyed wearing English suits. On one particular day, we were shopping for neckties, and as we looked, he asked me which one I thought was good. I perused the stack and picked one. It had a diamond-like pattern with little white dots. Then he smiled and said, "That's a good one."

To some, it may seem strange that a high Tibetan lama would appreciate material objects at all. However, his message through the Shambhala teachings was that we cannot hide from the world. He taught that genuine spirituality is living in the world and celebrating it, without being seduced or corrupted by it.

My father taught me that corruption is the result of an inability to relate to our own power. He said that when a culture becomes corrupt, it ceases to become *now*; it becomes past and future. My father felt that humanity was entering a period when we would inevitably create a world of corruption if people in corporations and governments were ignorant about the true source of human power.

In China, Confucius and Mencius introduced the principles of power in joining heaven and earth. "Heaven" was vast spaciousness—power that arose from the highest place, goodness. "Earth" was the resources at hand—nowness. It was humanity's duty to join these two in a harmonious society. This was called "cultivating the Way." The vehicle for doing this was virtue. Using patience not anger, exertion not laziness—virtue comes about from being on the spot. As my father put it, "You should have the honorable decency to keep your nowness. It is up to you."

In the current modern system, it seems that our vehicle is not virtue but materialism. Although we never lose basic goodness, under these circumstances, we have lost our heaven and earth. We are experiencing an air of instability and anxiety because our power is grounded in superficial principles. My father once said that money is mother's milk. Whatever money we have in our pocket we should appreciate and respect, because it is a representation of hard work that gives us an economic basis from which to do good. Endless accumulation is thwarting our attempts at happiness because our values are misguided. We all need food and clothing, but if we are to enjoy our wealth—yet not be dominated, seduced, and fooled by it—it is now more important than ever to reestablish the view that true value lies within, and that we are here to share that treasure.

How do we regard our money? Beyond the essentials, how do we invest it? By reflecting on our values, we can align them with our own true power. Goodness is not going to diminish, but if we do not link this internal force to our actions, it stands to be abused or forgotten. Power and wealth do not naturally corrupt humanity. What corrupts humanity is the inability to harness and ride its natural power and wealth. Riding our power is the ability to remain on our horse of goodness, secure in our worthy feeling. When doubt unseats us, we lose the ability to appreciate who and what we are. In turn, this makes us vulnerable to other sources of power, and we become easy to seduce—emotionally or ethically open to manipulation.

At this critical juncture, we must reexamine and redefine our relationship to currency. Clearly it is just paper and coins—or in the modern era, bits of digital information—but like anything else, it begins to pick up its own energy. Throughout history, it has often been associated with negative human qualities. Do we now feel that it has some magical power to bring happiness? Has our age fooled us into believing that once we possess money, we possess value? It has the power to make us rich, but does that wealth truly enrich us?

The character of any successful society comes down to confidence in its principles: The stronger the principles, the more robust the confidence and the more successful the society. A society based on deeper principles can see how to lay the ground for the future, while a society based upon shallow principles is easily manipulated, and therefore has an uncertain and tenuous future. In this light, if a society's trust is rooted in superficial values, then when the economy falters, trust falters; therefore the kindness falters, and the society falters.

Within this point lies the very purpose of enlightened society: A society that puts its trust in wakefulness is rooted in the deepest, most profound reality. In goodness we have tapped into the most stable currency on earth. From this treasure chest arise virtues that overcome corruption—the poverty of selfishness, greed, and fixation.

When I was with my father, whether we were eating, shopping, or just talking, our power and dignity were being maintained. That is how he taught me to relax with my own sense of integrity. With that approach, life is no longer a display of what we do not have. Rather, with enriching qualities of body, speech, and mind, we link our inner abundance to the world at large. We're no longer afraid to be generous, because we know the goodness is always there, and by rousing it in ourselves, we extend it to others. Therefore, whether we have wealth or not, the Shambhala antidote to chronic need, guilt, and emotional poverty is generosity and magnanimity.

How does this practice help us in daily life? In terms of the body, we groom ourselves well—wearing clean clothes, eating nourishing food, and keeping fit. We meditate daily, cultivating good posture and good habits, discarding unwholesome ways. This is how we begin to glimpse our own richness, which is peace and equanimity, and offer it to the world.

This experience gradually makes us less aggressive. Our senses take on a richer quality, with a strong sense of appreciation. We have mindfulness of our feelings. We begin to *feel* how we feel. Then we are able to make intelligent decisions about what to do with our emotions. In terms of speech, we use words eloquently, infusing them with truth. We value conversation and always have time for listening, which provides the space and warmth for growth. If we're not in a rush, we have the patience to let relationships unfold naturally.

In our minds, we have fearlessness, which is how we celebrate our lives, no matter what the situation. As my father would say, the warrior should not be afraid of wealth and power, nor should the warrior fear silence and boredom. In either situation, we know everything we need is already here, to be offered to the world. Because we're powered by confidence, we're not afraid to give up territory or to dare to take a leap if that's what is necessary to move forward. We also have humor, a sign of pliability and intelligence. Because we're connected to our wholesomeness, we're able to lighten up.

The notion of enlightenment is that no matter how dark the room is, even if it has been dark for thousands of years. as soon as someone lights a match, the room is illuminated. We have the tools to do this right here in our mind—the same mind that is reading this book. When we discover that mind and cultivate our discovery in a continuing way, our lives are driven by windhorse rather than drained by depression. We wake up every morning with confidence: "I have this treasure called awakened heart and mind, which is positive and strong. How am I going to apply it throughout my day?" Then we turn our mind to fearlessness, gentleness, and humor and decide to share those qualities throughout the day by bringing them into thought and action. In the evening, we can take a moment before sleep and reflect on what happened: "How did I use my power to enrich the world today?"

When we went on our shopping expeditions, my father was training me in just these points—how to keep my own inner value and infuse my environment with it, even while shopping. Then I learned how to be unafraid of the world and its beauty, how not to be seduced and fooled by material objects. When we do that, the material world becomes an expression of human goodness and confidence, as opposed to human weakness and vulnerability. If we can reprioritize our values and return to a natural balance that incorporates our worthiness, we will recognize that the true gold standard of humanity is goodness, from which confidence and virtue arise. This is how we will enrich the future of humanity.

19

EDUCATION

ONE AFTERNOON IN the mid-seventies, I asked my father where he was going. He said, "To start a school. Would you like to come along?" He was addressing an audience of young hippies, intellectuals, and spiritual seekers in Boulder, Colorado, all ready to change the world. It was certainly a festive and exuberant time. Little did they know that my father was there to create a culture of now-ness. To their surprise, he talked about the importance of not abandoning the mainstream. He asked them not to run away from society, but to engage with it. He even advised them to trade in their tie-dyed skirts, T-shirts, and jeans for business suits.

With that address, my father started a school that was

based on the Shambhala principle of basic goodness. The result of his effort is now Naropa University, the first accredited North American Buddhist-based institution of higher learning. The summer he began Naropa, my father was quoted as saying, "When East meets West, sparks will fly." Some felt that the sparks he spoke of signified an impending cultural clash, but I felt the sparks to be the Eastern and Western expressions of the same thing, which my father was trying to unify. In fact, the Latin root of the word *university* means "all turned into one." In Naropa, my father was attempting to create an education system where natural human curiosity and the wish to understand ourselves and our world could be nourished. It was an approach to learning based on innate wisdom. In Shambhala we teach methods for connecting to basic goodness, but there are many paths to this place. However, when my father arrived in the West, he found that religion and spirituality were becoming scarce. Even philosophy was thought to be a purely theoretical discipline, and the notion of wisdom had been relegated to intuition or probability. Yet receiving only knowledge leaves us with an incomplete feeling.

By starting the school, my father was not attempting to add a few more courses of spiritual development, but rather to introduce new building blocks for the modern mind. He knew that if we were going to address the world and its problems, we would have to start at the root, for how we feel about humanity is integrally tied to education.

The thirteenth-century rise of universities in Western culture is attributed to both the formation of large cities and the discovery of Aristotle's texts in Arabic, which were then translated into the European languages. Medieval Europe rediscovered its roots in ancient Greece, giving birth to the Renaissance. Universities became the new home of ancient wisdom and knowledge, slowly replacing monastic institutions. Thus, today's universities have their roots in educating the complete human being, teaching both knowledge and wisdom.

In Tibet, inspired by ancient India, the institutes of higher learning were monasteries. Much like ancient Greece, India was a place of rich cultural curiosity. Philosophy and metaphysics were not simply theoretical; they were the principles for a good human life. It is interesting to note that when Alexander the Great conquered parts of Asia, ancient India and Greece encountered each other. Apparently this led to the Greeks studying Hinduism and, even later, Buddhism. These Greeks became known as Bactrian Buddhists.

Thus, over the centuries, sparks have already flown more than once. Whether it involved ancient Greece, India, Tibet, or China, each occurrence provoked an exploration of the possibility of universal goodness. This discussion became the foundation of civilizations and, therefore, of educational systems. It was Petrarch who said, "It is more important to want the good than to know the truth." My father was saying that, in fact, the truth and the good are the same thing. The sparks that fly are the sparks of goodness.

My father was inspired by the constant search for meaning and truth in both East and West. In founding Naropa University, he was trying to introduce an educational system rooted in the worthiness of being. From his own upbringing, he knew that emphasizing human dignity as an educational foundation brings to students an inherent respect for themselves. The transfer of knowledge can then occur, and the discovery of wisdom is appreciated, which leads us to acknowledge the worthiness of others. If we doubt our own dignity, no matter how much education we receive, we will always feel inadequate.

My father's own education had been thorough and strict. It was not simply based on knowledge, but also on wisdom—"Training the complete human being," as he often said. Years later, he was still expressing gratitude toward his tutors and teachers, who had taught him, almost from infancy, about the great perfection that we humans are here to reflect. What if, from an early age, our own children were educated in this view?

When he came to the West, my father saw that much education here is rooted in the premise that there is an inherent fault to be fixed. Denying that people possess wisdom sucks the breath from life. We feel trapped, with no wonderment and curiosity. By the same token, until we appreciate our worthiness, all the freedom in the world will not satisfy us. Gaining outside knowledge becomes a constant reminder of the inner truth we do not know.

Goodness is based on appreciation—appreciating what we have. In addition, education is the process of developing our innate qualities so we have them to appreciate. My father's education involved gaining knowledge, but it also involved gaining wisdom. Knowledge is what we can learn as a trade skill in literature, science, or the arts. But wisdom is something uniquely human, and actually, it cannot be taught. Rather, it involves our ability to take a hint and pick up on the message spontaneously. Aristotle referred to this as "divine intelligence." It is the delight at the root of our being.

We all need both knowledge and wisdom. We need knowledge to feed and clothe ourselves in order to survive, and at the same time, there is an element of our being that yearns for some deeper, unfathomable inner principle in order to help us understand who we are and why we are alive. This is very clear in the simple questions of little children. Why do we have two arms, two legs, two eyes, and two ears? Why is the sky blue? The combination of knowledge and wisdom gives people the ability to remain on earth and at the same time touch the heavens.

Watching my own daughter grow, it is so clear that we all begin with an innate curiosity, sensitivity, and wonder at our magical and strange world. Children are naturally oriented toward learning. For most kids, it is inseparable from playfulness and joy. According to the Shambhala principle, education is the nourishing of this natural wish to learn. Unfortunately, all too often our educational systems hold the view that we are innately confused or disinterested. The resulting systems of teaching, testing, and assessment may squelch children's curiosity and close the door to wisdom.

In my own education, my father encouraged me to take pride in being human. His experience had taught him that when education is rooted in the view of inherent goodness, the student's yearning for wisdom and knowledge intensifies. Discipline and structure only increase their appetite, with each new challenge a further opportunity for them to manifest their strengths.

In modern education, with its orientation toward training us for our vocation, once we have received enough training, we stop learning. Even though education is meant to uplift us and help us reach our potential, it has also created a state of mind that is a cross between anxiety and complacency. With knowledge comes worry. The more information and knowledge we gain, the more there is to worry about. As our minds are filled with the endless scenarios of how things can go wrong, there is very little time to contemplate the ways in which we are good. Our wisdom becomes a whisper that is relegated to the realm of the theoretical, spiritual, or religious. Thus, modern education is at a crossroads.

How can we educate people so that they do not lose touch with their sensitivity and curiosity? If the education process does not help foster human goodness, part of our spirit withers away. When children are raised in an environment that does not encourage basic goodness and self-worth, their sense of self-identity becomes fragile and confused. This imbalance leads to unhappiness and aggression such as bullying, which naturally begins to affect society.

Our age is marked by the decline of traditional religions and the rise of science as the new religion. Educational institutions have become the main cathedrals of this new faith, and the modern world is essentially a servant to science. We question the validity of anything that has not been proven by science. Even spirituality has to be validated by science. Science has obviously been essential to the success and prosperity of humanity. In fact, the Shambhala principle advocates the constant exploration of intelligence. However, if science erodes trust in our own wisdom, that knowledge is not serving us well. How are we to distinguish between expanding ourselves with knowledge and limiting ourselves with knowledge?

In ancient Greece, India, and Tibet, philosophy and

spirituality were completely infused with reason and logic. Empirical analysis was integral to the spirit, and science had a deep respect for humanity. The two existed side by side with faith. Plato and Aristotle never saw any true dichotomy between the sciences and the spirit. Like Socrates, Naropa—the tenth-century Indian scholar for whom my father named his school—had a brilliant mind. He was always mixing education and life.

In Tibet, the natural sciences were essential to any full education, and gleaning knowledge about the body through the study of medicine was valued. At the same time, the ancients acknowledged the existence of both a human spirit and a human mind. They saw the need to educate these two simultaneously. However, in modern times, we have somehow created unnatural friction. We see spirituality as the opposite of logic and reason and, therefore, as the opposite of science and technology.

It is clear that the sciences are critical to our survival. But the handling of the spirit and mind are equally critical. If we are living in a world that is increasingly devoid of the spirit, our educational system is only servicing one aspect of humanity. Human wisdom, heart, and spirit are demoted and marginalized. Beyond the context of religion or spirituality, our inner needs are not being addressed. We experience this as a feeling of inadequacy.

As well, with the decline of the family, cultural ethics and decorum have slowly been abandoned. Therefore, we have created a paradoxical situation. Science and technology exist to enhance life, yet their energies threaten to bully out what makes life truly enjoyable—the edification of the human spirit. Once our basic physical needs are met, enjoying life involves fulfilling our spiritual and emotional necessities. If expressing these principles has no home in their education, where will our children learn to relate with them?

If science and technology tell us that human wisdom, heart, and spirit cannot be proven, we become suspicious of our own insights and experiences. We have no vocabulary or social settings in which to express how we feel and think. In fact, we moderns must hire people to pay attention and listen to accounts of our inner lives. How can we create an educational system that has genuine respect for body and mind, fact and feeling, empirical and elusive?

The interplay between knowledge and wisdom benefits both science and the humanities. If they become lopsided, both science and the humanities will lose. However, if this interplay remains strong, they will succeed. In order to survive, humanity needs faith, even if it is rooted in science. At this poignant time, science has revealed a fantastic array of knowledge for us to explore—understanding everything from the limits of outer space to the depths of the oceans, from the human body to our natural environment. With this explosion of knowledge, can we simultaneously release our wisdom into the universe and beyond?

It can happen if we can show our children the wisdom that arises when we encourage human worthiness.

How can we create enlightened society if we need proof of humanity's goodness? In that case, our educational process will be fighting a losing battle. As we seemingly gain knowledge, we will simultaneously lose wisdom. Scientific discoveries often arise due to intuition or hypothesis, the ability to reach into the unknown and come into contact with knowledge that allows the mind to extend even further. To shift the direction of the future, can we now couple intellect with wisdom? Including self-reflection in our daily ceremony is the perfect way for these two to meet.

As I returned with my father on that summer afternoon, he looked at me and said, "You have a lot to learn." I smiled and said, "I know."

20

UNCONDITIONAL HEALTHINESS

ONE DAY, I began sneezing. My father turned to me and asked what was wrong. I said, "I think I have hay fever." He looked at me and said, "We Tibetans don't get hay fever." I contemplated this. I thought it was a rather insensitive thing to say. There was no doubt a mixture of cultural pride and spiritual wisdom in his words. Tibetans come from a hearty stock, and it did seem slightly inconsequential to complain about hay fever to a man who had walked out of the Himalayas. I smiled and laughed at his answer. "That's better," he said.

My father told me that I needed to stop fighting the elements and relax. This required me to surrender my concept of hay fever and abruptly switch my allegiance to the present moment. Then my father transmitted a very important bit of psychosomatic wisdom: He told me I should trust my basic healthiness. He said that while sickness is part of life, sickness is not life, and that I should always approach sickness from the point of view of healthiness. I knew he knew what he was talking about, since in his travels, he had experienced starvation and frostbite, as well as several tropical diseases.

My father's approach to health was connected with the physical manifestation of basic goodness. He was saying that if I could leap beyond my convoluted thinking process, I would find that worthy feeling. At a psychophysical level, it is the notion of complete healthiness. Humanity is fundamentally healthy. If its nature were not fundamental health, the species could not survive.

The Shambhala principle thus advocates that at a physical level we are unconditionally healthy, and at a psychological level we are also unconditionally healthy. We are intact, and our nature as humans is profoundly good; otherwise, how could we experience the joy of a long run, or a child smiling? From this inherently good health, we have the power to make sound decisions.

Over the years, my father's words have begun to haunt me. As a modern culture, we are beginning to lose faith in the healthiness of humanity, which means we believe in a culture of unhealthiness. Because we have polluted and overpopulated the earth, air quality and the water supply are dwindling, and as technology threatens to overwhelm us, we will no doubt continue to encounter new illnesses and diseases, and therefore will need to develop more medicines.

On the one hand, this is a medical issue. On the other hand, it is a cultural issue. If humanity develops the attitude that unhealthiness is our nature, we will be more susceptible to illness, because just holding that attitude will weaken our immune systems. For myself, there have been times when I have felt sick and was able to feel better by changing the environment—by going to bed, or by associating with different people. Simply by creating a healthier environment, I created a healthier attitude also.

There are maladies far more serious than hay fever, but even when things seem incurably bad, we can remain incurably good. If this age of plague, famine, and war gains the upper hand, and we forget our goodness, we could find ourselves in a vulnerable position both physically and mentally. Our health care system is at a crossroads created by the confluence of economy, the environment, society, and health. Likewise, the health of our species naturally affects our relationship with the environment, the economy, and society. As these personal and social elements mix, they all melt within the cauldron of our personal well-being. The attempt to become more progressive with technology and information naturally takes a toll on our humanity.

It's a simple universal law that the more we create, the more we have to manage, and the more stress is placed on our mind and our body. If we are advancing at a rate that outpaces our ability to handle the accompanying stress, we need to self-reflect: Is this truly progress? Even though modern medicine seems almost miraculous, and taking pills might temporarily counteract the mounting pressure, the most beneficial approach for the future is to balance the stress equally with a sense of fundamental healthiness.

The word *health* indicates a feeling of being complete, in balance and in harmony, free of disease and suffering. It indicates vitality; the faculties are alive and working. Therefore, health is the life force within us that makes us human, and to have strong life force is a completely natural part of being human.

The Shambhala principle emphasizes a sense of health based on natural connectivity and interdependence. Being healthy and maintaining health is not related just to diet and exercise, but with how we eat, with whom we eat, and how we relate to our body through movement. Even if we eat healthy and organic food, if we are surrounded by an aggressive and speedy society and feel numb to our feelings, our total health is not being addressed. If personally or socially we are forgetting to nurture the human spirit, then naturally we will feel a dampening of the spirit in our health. We will begin to feel that we are somehow flawed, which decreases our self-esteem. This in turn affects our vitality, illness and disease increase, and we end up thinking that ill health—not fundamental healthiness—is natural.

In a society that encourages us to feel our natural healthiness, our relationship to life's natural challenges is more balanced. The Shambhala approach to healthiness begins at an inner level by being kind to ourselves: appreciating what we eat through mindfulness, exchanging with others through empathy, resting with our fears, and allowing our minds to have dreams. On the outer level, it encourages respect for human dignity. Even though we are all prone to being born, growing up, aging, sickness, and death, we can approach life's vicissitudes from the reference point of goodness, whether we are healthy or ill. In this way, basic goodness becomes our cosmic health care. Inevitably, we will become ill, but that does not prevent us from touching our basic goodness. The day does not have to be perfect in order for us to feel a sense of celebration. Thus, even illness becomes a way to discover our treasure, which allows us to celebrate being alive.

21

THE HUMAN RIGHTS OF GOODNESS

WHEN I ASKED my father if everybody has basic goodness, he gave me a long, hard stare and said, "Yes. Everyone *is* basic goodness." He punctuated this statement
further by adding, "It's everyone's right."

Concern with human rights threads throughout history. Especially since the Second World War, it has become a compelling issue. Our recognition of fundamental
rights such as access to clean water and education are further signs of humanity enlightening itself in an attempt to
meet every person's elemental needs. Where we are now
represents a further evolution of connectivity, and our
technology is helping us make global links. I believe this
modern development is a natural outgrowth of humanity
beginning to touch its own nature. At the same time, the

movement has evolved out of shock and horror at what humanity can do to itself. As a way to guard the future, it arose from a deep sense of fear.

Like many people, when I first heard the term "basic goodness," I immediately thought of a few people I knew. All of us have people in our lives who have harmed us in some way. And on a global level, what about the damage done by tyrants and other aggressive forces? How could such people possibly be good?

So when my father said that basic goodness is everyone's right, I had to rethink the meaning of the term. He was not simply referring to rights that protect us as individuals. Rather, he was talking about a state of being that cannot be questioned. It was clearly not conditioned by people's behavior, but pointed to a deep, fundamental openness—our natural health. If we have healthiness of mind, then even if we do have sickness of body, there's automatically less anger. Everyone has the right to feel his or her own goodness. The conventional human rights of sociopolitical freedom are a natural extension of that awareness.

My father personally experienced the horrors of war and genocide. That led to his bravery in declaring basic goodness. He felt that if this message was not proclaimed, humanity would continue to move toward a troubled future because our feelings about our nature would be unexamined and unresolved. Although it is necessary to protect human rights, he felt that laws governing these rights could be a positive declaration of human dignity that arises out of victory over aggression, rather than a negative protective agent that arises from fear.

I asked my father if he thought people would continue to do cruel and violent things. He replied that it appeared that they would. He went on to say that if humanity can remember its nature, cruel and violent behavior will be greatly reduced, even though there will always be trag-edies. Indeed, against a social backdrop of conviction in humanity's worthiness, such events will fuel our resolve to do better. He said that if we cannot agree on the nature of humanity, human violence will continue to escalate. Because it is fueling our fear, we will need to increase our vigilance and ferocity about maintaining human rights. The need to protect human rights is a sign of humanity's valor; at the same time, it reflects an elemental mistrust of humanity.

Historically, humanity's cruelty is clearly revealed in the aftermath of violence and destruction. Yet the sadness we feel at such times inevitably contains a ray of hope. Despite apparent atrocities, our goodness shines through. We see this in the story of the Indian monarch Ashoka. In the third century B.C.E., Ashoka's empire was one of the most powerful and sophisticated on earth. Its influence reached from Southeast Asia to the Middle East and parts of China. In terms of economic might, it was a superpower of its era. Then, in the state of Orissa in southeast India, Ashoka conducted a battle known as Kalinga. This savage war left more than 250,000 soldiers dead, as well as thousands of civilians and animals. It is said that when Ashoka observed the death and devastation, he saw the futility of warfare and wept. He then vowed never again to engage in war.

After the battle of Kalinga, Ashoka adopted Buddhism. Although it was a new religion at the time, he was moved by its message of peace and universal harmony. He established hospitals, rest areas, and rights for women. He erected pillars declaring ethics based on human dignity—essentially, the human rights of the day. His royal seal, the "lion capital"—a pillar with four lion heads—is to this day a symbol of India. Emperor Ashoka aspired to base the socioeconomic culture of his kingdom on the principle of goodness, which had a profound effect on all aspects of life. His wish shows the power of determining the direction we want our lives to take.

Continuing to consider human rights and happiness will inevitably lead us toward even greater sophistication in considering our own nature. To shift the direction of our planet, we must now be willing to experiment with the theory that within the speed and stress, we are good. If we doubt the power of human thought, we must remember that current important themes in the West—human rights, freedom, the relationship between the individual and the state—all stem from one person having had a theory about what it means to be human. We are under the influence of philosophers, writers, and visionaries coming to various conclusions through their thoughts and feelings. That is the point of the Shambhala principle: What humanity feels about itself is not without meaning. Now it is up to humanity to consciously decide for itself what it feels. Concrete changes can arise from our sense of self-worth, as they did in the time of Ashoka. The deeper and more durable the principle, the more resilient our global society.

22

THE NEW HUMAN MANDATE

"I HAVE DONE what I can; now you must do the rest." These were some of the final words my father uttered to me, more than a quarter of a century ago. Not only was he my father; he was my mentor, teacher, and friend. As well, he was a great thinker and a profoundly accomplished meditation master. He was a genuine friend to humankind—a humanitarian and visionary. In my tradition, he was what we call a bodhisattva warrior: a courageous being who dedicates his life to the welfare of others. In his last minutes of life, I sat next to him and held him. At the end, he stared directly into my eyes, and before the flame of life was extinguished, I felt him transmitting his last moments of wisdom. I was twenty-four years old.

Since that day, I have reflected on how he brought the Shambhala principle to the world, and how I must continue to wake people up to basic goodness.

He was only forty-eight years old when he passed, yet he had accomplished so much. He was raised in one of the last truly spiritual kingdoms on earth. He experienced life as it had existed centuries ago: no running water, no electricity. He grew up immersed in the minds of intellectually and spiritually accomplished masters. He read the great books of the East. When he left Tibet, he ventured into the busy, modern, and chaotic world of gas fumes, television, electricity, indoor heating, and a myriad of languages. Because he was determined to cut through conventional concepts about spirituality, he took off the flowing robes of a monk and put on the suit and tie of a businessman. He delved into the rich Western culture of philosophy, politics, and economics. He experienced some of the great minds of Western thought, as well as the countercultural generation. With everything from Tibetan horns high in the Himalayas to jazz and rock concerts in New York to newspaper and magazine articles, his passing was lamented worldwide.

After my father transmitted basic goodness to me, I looked at my mind and tried to understand the source of any doubts I had in this principle. Later, I realized that my hesitation did not stem simply from a personal lack of confidence; rather, my conflicting views stemmed from the collective history of the world that I had adopted. That is what finally allowed me to personally conclude that the essence of humanity is goodness.

Then I began to look at why so many of us have come to a negative conclusion about human nature. Thus I began my journey of examining how we ended up with our current feelings, thoughts, and opinions. I discovered that the notion of basic goodness is prevalent throughout history, even if it is expressed in divergent ways. In fact, it is the driving force behind humanity's wish to succeed.

This journey led me back to the beginning of Western thought, and even to Socrates and the pre-Socratic thinkers, for whom human nature was a constant theme. It became evident that the early Greeks' conclusion of innate human goodness had inspired the creation of Athens, as well as many enlightened approaches to life, such as democracy.

At a similar time in Asia, the Buddha undertook a journey of understanding human nature and the nature of humanity altogether. He taught that within each of us lies the seed of a profound awakening. Around the same time, in China, Mencius was advocating innate goodness as the core of human nature. Basic goodness did not emerge just in philosophy, but also in the ancient spiritual traditions, in which Jesus, Muhammad, Rumi, and Hindu teachers all advocated some basic principle of human goodness.

In terms of the human mind, one of the greatest lessons

I learned from my father was the importance of the present moment. The present moment determines what the future will bring, for the mind simply follows the tendencies that are established in the present. If our attitude in the present moment is negative, we are only setting up negative tendencies for the future. Conversely, if we engender positive aspects, we are setting up positive tendencies for the future. The power is in the present moment.

Meditation has taught me that we always have the opportunity to seize the moment. The greater trust we have in ourselves, and the more conviction we have in our goodness, the more strength we will have to seize it. With self-doubt and lack of conviction, our past negative actions gain momentum and the joy of the present is awash in doubt and fear. Then the future looks dismal. If we as humanity feel good about ourselves, we will grab this particular moment with great conviction before it washes away. Each of us holds human destiny in our hands. It will be completely determined by how the mind feels about itself.

Thus, at this critical juncture, we should put our hand on our chest and feel our beating heart. That heartbeat is the pulse of all humanity. It is good, it is pure, it is whole. It has always has been that way—and it always will be. If we can embody that heart of goodness, humanity will have an indestructible tool.

When my father told me many years ago that I would be the next sakyong, he explained that the sakyong principle had existed within the spiritual legacy of humanity, but that it did not currently exist. I did not fully understand this statement at the time, but through my own life, I have learned that we all have the seed of this legacy. In the words "I have done what I could; now you must do the rest," he was encouraging me to lead others on the trail he had blazed. In his own training, his teachers cultivated the principle of basic goodness. When this goodness was challenged by aggression, he was not dissuaded—he emerged in the modern world with his conviction not only intact, but even stronger. Now, in his last moments on earth, he was saying that I, too, must take this journey.

However, over the years, I have come to understand that he was not simply asking me to hold a position or title; rather, the notion of earth protector concerns humanity as a whole. My father had empowered me and trusted me with the responsibility of understanding, protecting, and transmitting basic goodness to others. So I trained in the view of basic goodness, tested it against life's challenges, and increased my confidence.

Subsequently, as I assumed the mantle of his responsibility, I became responsible for communities in both the East and the West. On a daily basis, I felt the constant challenge of my mandate. Looking back on my journey and the struggles therein, I recall that the lure of simply meditating in a cave and leaving the world behind has often been appealing. I have received a lifetime of profound instructions. However, in my heart I knew that solitary retreat was not my calling. In fact, I lacked the luxury to even think about abandoning my world.

A major transformation occurred when I realized that I was in a most fortunate position. Somewhere in the snowy mountain ranges of Tibet, this ember of goodness had been transmitted to my father. He carefully and courageously transported it across the highest mountains in the world. He placed it in my hand and in my heart.

Now I know that being an earth protector means protecting humanity's greatest treasure. The most dynamic way to do this is to awaken the goodness of others. As we awaken our faith in the spirit of human goodness, it will radiate out from our planet, inspiring and illuminating the entire universe. That is how we will shift the future of our species: We will all become earth protectors by creating enlightened society.

Even though my father was only one person in this world, his spirit demonstrated what bravery and human goodness can accomplish. His life has been a beacon and inspiration for me. Now I ask you to touch your heart, feel your courage, intelligence, and kindness, and join me in proclaiming the basic goodness of humanity. By doing this, we are unfurling humanity's new flag, our collective conviction in human worthiness, the force that will change the future of our planet.

acknowledgments

I started writing *The Shambhala Principle* after concluding one year of retreat, during which I had contemplated and meditated on the themes of basic goodness and enlightened society. The book could not have occurred without the strong blessings and memory of my father, as well as the support of my wife, the Sakyong Wangmo, and my daughter, Jetsun Drukmo, and the support and enthusiasm of the Shambhala community.

I began writing the book during a thunderstorm in Boulder, Colorado, and continued in France. It followed me to Nepal, and finally to Nova Scotia. Thus, even the writing of the book occurred in a transcultural environment, which feels appropriate to its subject.

A few individuals were key in the writing of *The Shambhala Principle*. I would like to thank Mr. Mark Whaley for his warmth, exertion, and patience, and Mr. James Thorpe, who remained ever cheerful and quiet. Thanks to Mr. Adam Lobel—who became a great inspiration—especially for our fascinating discussions regarding the rich field of Western philosophy, and for his ample insight, open-mindedness, and cheerfulness. Thanks to Mr. Richard Reoch, who was ever supportive and perpetually encouraging about the need for this book, and to Mr. Josh Silberstein, for his enthusiasm and support. Thanks to Dr. Mitchell Levy, for his important feelings and insights about health; to Mr. John Rockwell, for his vigilant dedication; and to Mr. Gaylon Ferguson, for his enthusiasm regarding Confucian thought.

As well, reading the work of Pierre Hadot, the French philosopher and historian, came at an auspicious time while I was writing this book.

I would also like to thank my agent, Mr. Reid Boates, for his tenacity, and Mr. Gary Jansen and the staff of Harmony Books for having faith in this project and determination to publish it.

Finally, I would like to thank my editor, Emily Hilburn Sell, who has supported me in the writing of many books. I was especially moved and touched by her dedication to the completion of this one, as she saw the importance and necessity of the message of basic goodness at this time.

May the Shambhala principle become the guiding force for the future of humanity.

shambhala in the world

Shambhala is a global network of people from all walks of life, dedicated to the principle that the fundamental nature of every human being is basic goodness.

The Shambhala teachings on human dignity have been translated into more than a dozen major languages in live teachings, recordings, books, and online broadcasts. More than 100,000 people in 94 countries have attended in-depth programs to discover the principles of Shambhala.

For an introduction to Shambhala, with links to its worldwide network, please visit www.shambhalanews.com.

ABOUT THE AUTHOR

SAKYONG MIPHAM is the head of the Shambhala lineage, which is grounded in the power of creating enlightened society in everyday life. With a unique blend of Eastern and Western perspectives, he teaches this way of social transformation throughout the world. In addition, he extends his vision to a number of humanitarian projects in Asia and the West. He is the author of the bestselling titles *Running with the Mind of Meditation, Ruling Your World,* and *Turning the Mind into an Ally.*

For more information, visit www.sakyong.com.